Landscapes of
LANZAROTE
a countryside guide

Noel Rochford

SUNFLOWER
BOOKS

Dedicated to Augustín Pallarés Padilla

First published 1989 by
Sunflower Books
12 Kendrick Mews
London SW7 3HG, UK

Verode

ISBN 0-948513-48-9

Important note to the reader

I have tried to ensure that the descriptions and maps in this book are error-free at press date. The book will be updated, where necessary, whenever future printings permit. It will be very helpful for me to receive your comments (sent in care of the publishers, please) for the updating of future printings. I also rely on those who use this book — especially walkers — to take along a good supply of common sense when they explore. Conditions change fairly rapidly on Lanzarote, and **storm damage or bulldozing may make a route unsafe at any time.** If the route is not as I outline it here, and your way ahead is not secure, return to the point of departure. **Never attempt to complete a tour or walk under hazardous conditions!** Please read carefully the notes on pages 7 to 13, as well as the introductory comments at the beginning of each tour and walk (regarding road conditions, equipment, grade, distances and times, etc). Explore **safely**, while at the same time respecting the beauty of the countryside.

Photographs by the author
Maps by John Theasby and Pat Underwood
Drawings by Sharon Rochford
Printed and bound in the UK by A Wheaton and Co Ltd, Exeter
D5/KH

✿ Contents _____

Foreword   4

Preface   5
  Acknowledgements   6
  Useful books   6

Introduction   7
  Getting about on the island   7
  Picnicking   7
  Touring   8
  Walking   9
    Dogs and other nuisances   10
    Weather   10
    Where to stay   11
    What to take   11
  Spanish for walkers and motorists   12
  A country code for walkers and motorists   13

Picnic suggestions   14

Car tours   16
  The sights of the north (Tour 1)   16
  Timanfaya and the southern beaches (Tour 2)   25

Walks   31
  1 Around La Graciosa   31
  2 Risco de Famara   35
  3 Máguez • Casas la Breña • Yé   39
  4 Mala • Presa de Mala • Ermita de las Nieves • Teguise   43
  5 Mancha Blanca • Playa de la Madera • Tinajo   47
  6 Uga • Montaña Guardilama • La Montañeta • Mácher
     • Puerto del Carmen   50
  7 Yaiza • Atalaya de Femés • Yaiza   55
  8 La Hoya • El Convento • La Hoya   58
  9 Playa Blanca • Playa de Papagayo • Barranco Parrado
     • Maciot • Playa Blanca   62

Index   68

Touring map   after Index

Transport timetables   on touring map

Town plans   on touring map

Teguise

 # Preface

Within just a few years, Lanzarote has grown from a quiet, relatively unknown tourist resort to an island buzzing with some 600,000 tourists annually. Fortunately, these visitors are confined to three fairly small areas, and the rest of the island remains blissfully rural and unspoilt.

Few holidaymakers realise that Lanzarote has more to offer than just beaches and sunshine. I was sceptical. When my publisher suggested Lanzarote for my next book, I felt sure that I was doing penance for past manuscripts. But a pleasant surprise awaited me.

This fascinating 797-square-kilometre island is truly extraordinary. Its fate was decided some two and one-half centuries ago, when the largest volcanic eruption in recorded history took place, leaving a strange and alluring countryside in its wake — a landscape littered with volcanoes and dark streams of jagged lava. This is the backdrop to nearly every scene on the island, and intriguing sights abound, as you can see from the photographs in this book.

If you were to suggest walking on Lanzarote to most visitors, they would think you mad. "Where is there to walk?" But I can think of no better place in the Canary Islands for just strolling. No doubt 'serious' walkers will find Tenerife and Gran Canaria, for example, more challenging, but ramblers will be in their element on Lanzarote. Each of the walks in this book takes you to a different corner of the island and shows you a scenically-different outlook. But if walking is not your favourite pastime, then *do* rent a vehicle of sorts and explore on wheels. Use the book to reach places off the beaten track and see another face of Lanzarote.

At present all eyes are on this island. Will it indeed set an example in preservation, or will it follow in the footsteps of Tenerife and Gran Canaria, falling prey to the concrete of greedy developers? Fortunately, Lanzarote has one advantage over the other islands. It is the home of the well-known artist-designer — and, more importantly, conservationist — César Manrique. Together with his supporters, he is working to preserve the island's environmental heritage.

I hope this new addition to the *Landscapes* Series convinces you that there is much more to Lanzarote than beaches and sunshine.

Acknowledgements
My thanks to the following people, who helped me with the preparation of the material on Lanzarote:

Señor Francisco Ortega, Director, Patronato Insular de Turismo de Lanzarote;

Servicio Geográfico del Ejercito, Madrid, for permission to adapt their maps;

Señores Carlos Gutierrez Gutierrez and Norberto Palomino Gallego, for additional military maps;

ICONA;

Jackie, for her errands.

Very special thanks to Augustín Pallarés Padilla for invaluable suggestions and for hours spent answering my questions; and to my sister Sharon, for her splendid drawings.

Finally, thanks to my family, friends, and publishers, who always support my work and travels.

Useful books

Bramwell, D and Bramwell, Z *Wild Flowers of the Canary Islands.* Stanley Thornes Ltd.

Bramwell, D and Bramwell, Z *Historia Natural de las Islas Canarias.* Editorial Rueda.

Vicente Araña and Juán Carracedo, *Los volcanes de las Islas Canarias, II: Lanzarote y Fuerteventura* (with English text). Editorial Rueda.

Carlos Javier Taranilla, *Fuerteventura.* Editorial Everest.

Prickly pear

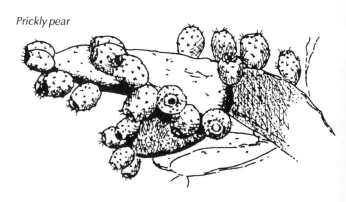

❀ Introduction ⎯⎯⎯⎯

Getting about on the island

The best way to get around Lanzarote is by **hired car**. This can be very economical, especially when you hire a car for a few days or a week. **Taxis** are only economical if shared, and all fares should be ascertained in advance. *Note: Never* leave anything of value in your car. Lock your personal belongings in the boot, or carry them with you. Thefts from cars are not uncommon. Always try to park where there are other cars and people are about.

    Coach tours are easy to arrange and get you to all the tourist points of interest, but never off the beaten track. The **local bus service** is very limited outside Puerto del Carmen and Costa de Teguise; it serves the school children and villagers. Most of the walks in this book can be reached by local bus, however — with departures from Arrecife. **Bus timetables** are shown on the touring map. *Don't* rely solely on these, however. As soon as you arrive on the island, update these timetables by getting 'first-hand' information from the *bus station* (it's best *not* to rely on tourist office handouts). See town plans (with the touring map) for bus stops and stations in both Arrecife and Puerto del Carmen. The buses may run late, but you should *always arrive about fifteen minutes early*. In the Arrecife bus station it will take you that long to find out *which one* is your bus!

Picnicking

Picnicking isn't one of Lanzarote's strong points. Shade is the biggest problem — there are not many trees on the island! Nor are there any 'organised' picnic sites, as there are on other Canary Islands. If you have just one day for picnicking, don't miss Picnic 2 (Risco de Famara). I think this is one of the loveliest and most memorable places to enjoy a picnic in the entire archipelago.

On pages 14 and 15 you will find my suggestions for eight lovely picnic spots, together with all the information you need to reach them. *Note that picnic numbers correspond to walk numbers*; thus you can quickly find the general location on the island by referring to the pull-out touring map (where the walk locations are shown in white). Most of the spots I've chosen are very easy to reach, and I outline transport details (🚌 = bus information; 🚗 = car or taxi parking), walking times, and views or setting. Beside the picnic title, you'll also find a map reference: the exact location of the picnic spot is shown on this large-scale *walking* map by the symbol **P**. Some of the picnic areas are also illustrated; if so, the photograph reference follows the map reference.

Please glance over the comments before you start off on your picnic: if some walking is involved, remember to wear sensible shoes and to **take a sunhat** (☉ = picnic in full sun). It's a good idea to take along a plastic groundsheet as well, in case the ground is damp.

If you are travelling to your picnic by bus, be sure to verify departure times in advance. Although there are timetables in this book, they *do* change from time to time, without prior warning. **If you are travelling to your picnic by car**, be extra vigilant off the main roads.

All picnickers should read the country code on page 13 and go quietly in the countryside. *Buen provecho!*

Touring

Hiring a vehicle is such good value on Lanzarote that it would be a pity not to take advantage of it. Do shop around first, however, while at the same time bearing in mind that cheapest is not always best! Always check your vehicle in advance and point out any existing dents, scratches, etc. Ask for all the conditions and insurance cover in writing, in English. Check to make sure you have a sound spare tyre and all the necessary tools. Be sure to get the office *and the after-hours* telephone numbers of the hire firm and carry them with you. If you're not 100% happy about the car, don't take it. Finally, make a note of exactly what you're signing for, if you pay by credit card.

You *can* tour Lanzarote in just one day without missing any of the main sights (indicated with a ★ in the touring notes and on the touring map) ... as long as you make a *very* early start.

The touring notes are brief: they contain little history or information readily available in tourist office leaflets (which you can obtain free of charge). The main tourist centres and towns are not described either, for the same reason. Instead, I concentrate on the 'logistics' of touring: times and distances, road conditions, and seeing places many tourists miss. Most of all I emphasise possibilities for walking and picnicking. While some of the references to picnics off the beaten track (indicated by the symbol *P* in the touring notes) may not be suitable during a long car tour, you may see a landscape that you would like to explore at leisure another day, when you've more time to stretch your legs.

The large fold-out touring map is designed to be held out opposite the touring notes and contains all the information you will need outside the towns. The tours have been written up starting from Puerto del Carmen, but you can join them from other points quite easily. **Town plans** with exits for motorists are on the touring map. Remember to allow plenty of time for **visits**, and to take along **warm clothing** as well as some food and drink, in case you are delayed. The **distances** quoted in the notes are *cumulative* from the departure point. A **key to symbols** used in the touring notes on pages 16 to 30 is on the touring map.

All motorists should read the country code on page 13 and go quietly in the countryside. *Buen viaje!*

Walking

While Lanzarote may not be the destination you might choose, were you planning a walking holiday, you will be as surprised as I was to find what this island has to offer walkers and nature lovers.

The walks in this book cover a good cross-section of the island. Do them all, and you will *almost* know Lanzarote inside-out. *Almost* — because, in a very commendable attempt to preserve the beauty of the island, the government will not permit you to explore the Timanfaya National Park on your own; you'll have to join the coach-trippers.

There are walks in this book for everyone. To choose a walk that appeals to you, you might begin by looking at the touring map inside the back cover. Here you can see at a glance the overall terrain, the roads, and the location of the walks. Flipping through the book, you will see that there is at least one photograph for every walk. Having selected one or two potential excursions from the map and the photographs, turn to the relevant walk. At the top of the page you will find planning information: distance/time, grade, equipment, and how to get there. If the grade and equipment specifications are beyond your scope, don't despair! *There's almost always a short or alternative version of a walk,* and in most cases these are far less demanding. *If you want a really easy walk, you need look no further than the picnic suggestions on pages 14 and 15.* For the hardy among you, look no further than Walk 2; this will get you huffing and puffing!

When you are on your walk, you will find that the text begins with an introduction to the overall landscape and then quickly turns to a detailed description of the route. The **large-scale maps** (generally 1:40,000 or 1:50,000) have been specially annotated to show key landmarks. Times are given for reaching certain points in the walk. **Note: I am a very fit, very fast walker!** So if you are a beginner, or if you prefer a more leisurely pace, a walk may **take you more than twice as long!** The most imporant factor is *consistency* of times, and I suggest that you compare your pace with mine on one or two short walks, before you set off on a long hike. Don't forget to take bus connections into account!

Note that roads and tracks on the walking **maps** correspond to those on the touring map. **Scale** of miles and **north/south** orientation is included on each map. Below is a key to the **symbols** used to indicate landmarks:

⌖	best views	*P*	picnic spot (see page 7)
✝/✚	church, chapel/shrine	❣	danger; danger of vertigo!
◀●	spring, tank, etc	🚗	car parking
□□□	habitations	■	building in the text
⚡	pylon, wires	▬	walls (usually stone)

Dogs and other nuisances

Dogs are a nuisance, that's for sure! They can recognise a softie a mile off, and they would follow me to the end of the walk. No amount of threatening or abuse deterred them. That's the only 'nuisance' on Lanzarote.

Weather

With an average annual temperature of 21°C and less than 140mm (5½ inches) of rain per year, Lanzarote has about 125 days of sunshine. You can't go wrong on a winter holiday here. You may strike a few bad days, but the only place where the weather could ruin your day would be in the north, where low cloud might prevent you from appreciating those superb seascapes. It would be very rare for rain to disrupt an entire day on the island. Rain usually lasts for only an hour or two, and then the sun shines again. Fortunately for walkers, there are some cool and cloudy days — these are not as uncommon as the tourist brochures would lead you to believe. The winter months (November to March) are best for walking, but even then the days can be hot.

A few facts and figures: Temperatures average between 14-21°C in winter and 18-28°C in summer, with humidity reaching between 60-70%. Good news for windsurfers: Lanzarote is a relatively windy island, with the *alisio* (trade winds) blowing for much of the year, and the mean average water temperature is 20°C.

In spring and summer there are occasional days when a warm wind blows from Africa, bringing with it fine particles of dust. It's not very pleasant, as the temperatures can be quite high, but it only lasts a few days.

Where to stay

Most of you will be staying in one of three places: Puerto del Carmen (the tourist capital), Costa de Teguise (smaller and classier), or Playa Blanca (still in its infancy). Any of these bases is fine, provided that you have a hired vehicle. However, if walking is more important to you than is the beach, and you are not planning to hire a car, it would be best to base yourself in Arrecife, from where you can easily get to all the walks by local bus. Puerto del Carmen *does* have a regular bus connection with Arrecife, but bear in mind that the service returning *from* Puerto del Carmen to Arrecife is not always strictly to the timetable. Costa de Teguise has a limited service connecting with Arrecife, and the service from Playa Blanca to the capital is only once a day each way.

All three tourist centres are within reach of at least three walks in the book, and you will find that by sharing a taxi one way and taking a local bus for the other part of the route (since you can usually get a bus at least one way), the cost for getting to and returning from walks is not high.

What to take

If you're already on Lanzarote when you find this book, and you don't have any special equipment such as walking boots or a rucksack, you can still do some of the walks — or buy yourself some equipment in one of the sports shops. Don't attempt the more difficult walks without the proper gear. For each walk in the book, the *minimum* equipment is listed.

Please bear in mind that I've not done *every* walk in this book under *all* weather conditions. Use your good judgement to modify my equipment list according to the season! You may find the following checklist useful:

walking boots (which *must* be broken-in and comfortable)

waterproof rain gear (outside summer months)

long-sleeved shirt (sun protection)

bandages and band-aids

plastic plates, cups, etc

anorak (zip opening)

spare bootlaces

sunhat

insect repellant

small rucksack

up-to-date transport timetables

lightweight water containers

extra pair of socks

long trousers, tight at the ankles

protective sun cream

knives and openers

2 lightweight cardigans

plastic groundsheet

whistle

compass

torch

Spanish for walkers and motorists

In the tourist centres you hardly need know any Spanish. But out in the countryside, a few words of the language will be helpful, especially if you lose your way.

Here's an — almost — foolproof way to communicate in Spanish. First, memorise the few short key questions and their possible answers, given below. Then, when you have your 'mini-speech' memorised, always ask the many questions you can concoct from it **in such a way that you get a "sí" (yes) or "no" answer.** *Never* ask an open-ended question such as "Where is the main road?". Instead, ask the question and then *suggest the most likely answer yourself*. For instance: "Good day, sir. Please — where is the path to Máguez? *Is it straight ahead?"* Now, unless you get a "sí" response, try: *"Is it to the left?"* If you go through the list of answers to your own question, you will eventually get a "sí" response, and this is more reassuring than relying solely on sign language.

Following are the most likely situations in which you may have to practice your Spanish. The dots (...) show where you will fill in the name of your destination. Ask a local person — perhaps someone at your hotel — to help you with place name pronunciation.

Asking the way
Key questions

English	Spanish	Pronunciation
Good day, sir (madam, miss).	Buenos días, señor (señora, señorita).	**Boo**-eh-nohs **dee**-ahs, sen-**yor** (sen-**yor**-ah, sen-yor-**ee**-tah).
Please — where is	Por favor — dónde está	**Poor** fah-**vor** — **dohn**-day es-**tah**
the road to ...?	la carretera a ...?	lah cah-reh-**teh**-rah ah ...?
the footpath to...?	la senda de ...?	lah **sen**-dah day ...?
the way to ...?	el camino a ...?	el cah-**mee**-noh ah ...?
the bus stop?	la parada?	lah pah-**rah**-dah?
Many thanks.	Muchas gracias.	**Moo**-chas **gra**-thee-ahs.

Possible answers

English	Spanish	Pronunciation
here?	aquí?	ah-**kee**?
there?	allá?	ayl-**yah**?
straight ahead?	todo recto?	**toh**-doh **rayk**-toh?
behind?	detrás?	day-**tras**?
right?	a la derecha?	ah lah day-**ray**-chah?
left?	a la izquierda?	ah lah eeth-kee-**er**-dah?
above?	arriba?	ah-**ree**-bah?
below?	abajo?	ah-**bah**-hoh?

Asking a taxidriver to take you somewhere and return for you, or asking a taxi driver to meet you at a certain place and time

English	Spanish	Pronunciation
Please —	Por favor —	**Poor** fah-**vor** —
take us to ...	llévanos a ...	l-**yay**-vah-nohs ah...
and return	y venga buscarnos	ee **vain**-gah boos-**kar**-nohs
at (*place*) at (*time*).	a ... a ... .*	ah (*place*) ah (*time*).*

Just point out the time on your watch.

A country code for walkers and motorists

- **Do not light fires.**
- **Do not frighten animals.** The goats and sheep you may encounter on your walks are not tame.
- **Walk quietly** through all hamlets and villages.
- **Leave all gates just as you find them.** Although you may not see any animals, the gates *do* have a purpose — generally to keep goats or sheep in (or out of) an area.
- **Protect all wild and cultivated plants.** Don't try to pick wild flowers or uproot saplings. Obviously fruit and other crops are someone's private property and should not be touched. *Never walk over cultivated land.*
- **Take all your litter away with you.**
- **Walkers — *Do not take risks!*** This is the most important point of all. Do not attempt walks beyond your capacity, and do not wander off the paths described here if there is any sign of mist or if it is late in the day. **Do not walk alone**, and *always* tell a responsible person *exactly* where you are going and what time you plan to return. Remember, if you become lost or injure yourself, it may be a long time before you are found. On any but a very short walk close to villages, be sure to take a compass, whistle, torch, extra water and warm clothing — as well as some high-energy food, like chocolate. Read and re-read the important note on page 2, as well as the guidelines on grade and equipment for each walk you plan to do!

Vinagrera

Picnic suggestions
1 LA GRACIOSA (map page 33)

by : 20-25min on foot. Ferry from Orzola to La Graciosa.
Off the ferry, skirt the waterfront to your left and continue around in front of and through the houses on the shore. Beyond the houses come to a superb beach and shortly after, a tidal lagoon. It's a fantastic spot, from where you look across to the impressive Risco de Famara (see Picnic 2).❂

2 RISCO DE FAMARA (map page 40, photographs pages 17 and 37)

by 🚗 *only:* 5-10min on foot. Park by the side of the road, 1.5km southwest of the Mirador del Río: Descending off the plateau, you come into cultivated fields. You'll see two derelict stone buildings set just below the side of the road. A dyke (a natural wall of rock) cuts across to the right directly behind them and, immediately beyond it, a track forks off right into the fields (alongside the dyke). Turn off onto the track and follow it to the end — or, if the track is too rough, park alongside the buildings.
Sit on the ledge of the cliff, below the track, and overlook the Mirador del Río vista — now you'll have the view all to yourself. No other picnic site on the island matches this one. Cliffs provide the only shade. ❂

3 MAGUEZ (map page 40, photograph page 22)

by 🚌: 30-35min on foot. Bus to Máguez.
by 🚗 : 20-25min on foot. On entering Máguez *from the north,* you encounter a fork in the road: bear left and, a few hundred metres/yards along, see a track bearing off to the left. Park on the side of the road here, without obstructing traffic.

Set off along the farm track, following the notes at the bottom of page 39 up to where the text reads 'just over 20min from Máguez ... we cross an intersection'. Here you can picnic on the grassy hillock above. There is a lovely view over the cultivated slopes down to the east coast, and Montaña Corona stands just behind you. ❂

4 PICO DE LAS NIEVES (map page 44)

by 🚗 *only:* 0-5min on foot. Park by the chapel at Pico de las Nieves, off the GC700.
Picnic anywhere on the top of the crest. The views across the centre of the Lanzarote and out to its neighbouring islands are magnificent. ❂

American aloe

6 MONTAÑA GUARDILAMA (map page 53, photographs pages 51, 53, 54)

by 🚌: 35-40min on foot. Bus to Uga.

by 🚗: 5-15min on foot. Turn off the Uga—Teguise road some 600m/yds past the junction north of Uga, onto the first track forking off east. Park off the side of the road at the entrance to the track; don't block the track. If you travel by jeep, you can drive up to the pass (this would take 40 minutes on foot).

Use the notes on pages 50- 52 to reach the pass, or go as far as you wish up the track. You have a superb view over the dark Geria Valley — quite a sight when the vines are coming into leaf. ❁

Lavandula pinnata

7 ATALAYA DE FEMES (map page 56, photograph page 57)

by 🚗 only: 30-40min on foot. Park in Femés.
Use the map for Walk 7, page 56. Follow the dirt track that leaves from behind the church and climbs the Atalaya de Femés. Picnic off the track above the first crater (from where your views will be limited), or carry on to the summit another 15 minutes further up. From there you will have an excellent view of the volcanoes of Timanfaya and the south of the island — as well as the northern part of Fuerteventura. Note that this is a strenuous climb, and it can be very windy and cool! ❁

8 JANUBIO (map page 60, photographs pages 59, 60)

by 🚌: 40-45min on foot. Bus to La Hoya.
by 🚗: 5-10min on foot. Turn off the Playa Blanca road onto the track signposted 'Playa', some 800m/yds beyond the junction for El Golfo. If approaching from Puerto del Carmen, this is the *second* track off right. Park above the beach.
Either picnic on this black sand beach or follow the walk notes on page 59 to head along the coastline to the left. There you'll find a choice spot amidst the rock fringing the shore. The beautiful rock pools lie between 40-50 minutes along. ❁

9 PLAYA DE PAPAGAYO (map pages 62-63, photograph page 64)

by 🚗 only: 0-5min on foot. Follow the gravel road east out of Playa Blanca (there are no signposts, and sections of road are under construction). Playa de Papagayo lies at the end of the main gravel road, 6km out (ignore the numerous branch-offs). Park around the hamlet above the beach.
Expect company here: Playa de Papagayo is mentioned in all the guides. There are good spots in the cove or on the rocky promontory to the right of the beach. Punta del Papagayo, less than 10 minutes beyond the hamlet, is always quiet. This point is usually windy. Playa de Puerto Muelas and the other beaches lining the coast also make splendid picnic spots. ❁

❁ Reminder: Little or *no* shade!

1 THE SIGHTS OF THE NORTH

Puerto del Carmen • Tahiche • Arrieta • Jameos del Agua • Cueva de los Verdes • Orzola • Mirador del Río • Haría • Teguise • La Caleta • Mozaga • Puerto del Carmen

140km/87mi; about 3h30min driving; Exit A from Puerto del Carmen

On route: **P** (see pages 14-15) 2, 3, 4; Walks 2, 3, 4

Roads are generally good, but often narrow. The road from Cueva de los Verdes to the GC710 (3km) is exceedingly narrow. Some motorists may find the roads around the Mirador del Río unnerving — especially near the Famara cliffs: there is at present no roadside railing. Cloud and mist are not infrequent in the northern hills, and visibility can be reduced to almost zero! Look out for livestock on the roads and for pedestrians in the villages. A slow speed is recommended for these roads. Note: There is only one petrol station between Arrieta and Mozaga — some 90km. Note also that some petrol stations are closed on Sundays and holidays. Arrecife is not included in this tour because it is well served by public transport and may be visited another day.

Important: *Although driving time is only three and one-half hours, allow an entire day for this tour if you want to visit all the tourist attractions.*

Opening hours:
Jameos del Agua: 11.00-19.30 daily
Cueva de los Verdes: 11.00-18.00 daily
Museo Sacro de Haría: 11.00-13.00 daily
Mirador del Río (bar): 11.00-19.00 daily
Castillo de Santa Bárbara: 10.00-18.00 daily
Palacio de Spinola: 10.00-13.00 and 16.00-18.00 daily

Outside of the Timanfaya National Park, the northern part of Lanzarote is the most scenically interesting. As you follow this tour, winding your way around and over the northern massif, you'll encounter the extraordinarily beautiful colours, shapes and textures that create the landscape canvas of Lanzarote. You'll need lots of film for your camera! Cueva de los Verdes — a vast volcanic tube measuring one kilometre in length, may be the most intriguing cave you've ever seen. You'll also learn who César Manrique is and what he means to the island — or, rather, what his native land means to him.

We leave Puerto del Carmen by heading north on the Avenida de las Playas (Exit A). On joining the main south road (GC720) bear right and, 4km along — just beyond a petrol station — turn off onto the circular road that skirts Arrecife. Next we turn off onto the GC700 and head for Tahiche/Teguise. Now the tour really begins.

At **Tahiche** (20km ✖) we take the GC710 for Orzola, passing through an open flat countryside pierced by prominent isolated hills. Approaching the Moorish-flavoured village of **Guatiza** (▲▲ 29km) we come into cultivated fields and gardens squared off by stone

16

walls. The village itself is swallowed up amidst fields of prickly pear. Leaving the village, pass the cactus garden (**Jardín de Cactus★**; still under construction at press date) on your right. A well-preserved windmill stands above it. Soon the entire plain is taken over by prickly pear. Farmed pricky pear is an unusual sight — normally we see it growing wild. The cochineal insect is bred on these

The fabulous setting of the Mirador del Río (Tour 1). The cliff is the famous Risco de Famara — see Walk 2.

plants: the female lives off the juice of the cactus leaf, and after three months is harvested and dried in the sun. Today cochineal is used as colouring in lipsticks, toothpastes, and some drinks — Campari, for instance. The dye was once important in the carpet industry and, during the last century, was a major money-earner for Lanzarote.

Off the sea-plain you look up into ridges that trail off the northern hills. **Mala** (32km ✕; starting point for Walk 4), another spacious farming village, follows. The 'Lanzarote colours' can be seen in the white façades and green doorways and window shutters of the houses. Passing **Arrieta** (37km 🚊✕🛆), a small seaside village built along the rocky shore, head straight through the junction. Then bear right immediately for Jameos del Agua and Cueva de los Verdes. A few minutes before you reach the turn-off to Jameos del Agua, you pass **Punta Mujeres** (38km ✕), a tight cluster of dwellings with more than its fair share of restaurants. Some 4km from Arrieta we branch off for **Jameos del Agua★** (42km ✕), one of the island's most-frequented tourist attractions. This enchanting cave is the result of two opposing forces — man and nature. A splendid compromise has been reached: the eruption of Montaña Corona is responsible for the natural element;

In Timanfaya National Park (Car tour 2): the Montañas del Fuego ('Fire Mountains') create a unique land-scape, rich in volcanic hues and textures. In order to preserve the beauty of this national park, tourists are not allowed to drive through the area on their own. But the coach tour that takes you through the park is a must for every visitor to Lanzarote.

César Manrique is the man. The cave has been skillfully transformed into a night club, maintaining as much natural décor as possible. Penetrating into the depths of the cave, you come to a large crystal-clear sea-pool. Shiny objects on the floor of the pool catch your eye: they are tiny white blind crabs (*Munidopsis poliforma*), unique to the sea world. You ascend to a large opening in the ground and a swimming pool set in a rock garden (in Jameos del Agua) bursting with colour (see photograph page 20).

Returning to the main road, we cross it and head up to the **Cueva de los Verdes★**, 1km away. The entrance to the cave remains obscure — no ticket office, souvenir shops or stalls scar the place. Thanks to, guess who? Only one of the seven kilometres of this vast complex of tunnels is open to the public. With a guide, you wind down through low, narrow passageways and emerge into enormous cool chambers — one of them an auditorium with perfect acoustics. The Guanches sought refuge in these caves whenever there were pirate raids. The caves were created when streams of molten lava solidified into a tunnel, and the crust outside cooled faster than the internal flow.

Back on the GC710, turn left for Orzola. Following the coast, we run along the edge of Malpais ('Badlands') de la

*Jameos del Agua — like the Mirador del Río, one of César Manrique'.
fine creations.*

Corona — an expansive undulating plateau of lava
carpeted in a thick mat of greenery. Patches of sand and a
couple of sandy coves embraced in the rocky shoreline
break up the lava flow. Soon see the table-topped island of
Alegranza over to your right — and the north of La
Graciosa. Rocky reefs create lagoons along the shoreline,
and these are ideal for swimming.

Orzola (53km ▲✕ and ⛴ to La Graciosa), at present
an ordinary fishing village, is all set for a 'face-lift'. The
Famara massif rises up into a bold block of hills in the
background, standing guard over the little port. Here's
where you catch the ferry, if you're planning to do Walk 1
or picnic on La Graciosa.

Now making for the Mirador del Río, we climb inland,
still circling the *malpais* on a narrow winding road. A
wavy blanket of greenery, pierced by rocky outcrops,
stretches below. We rejoin the GC710 at the foot of
Montaña Corona — a massive sharp-rimmed crater that
dominates the north of the island — and ascend to the
right. Thick stone walls soon take over the countryside;
their precision transforms the fields into a work of art. An
imposing solitary villa, Torrecilla de Domingo, rises up
out of this maze of walls, crowning a hilltop in the
shadows of Montaña Corona (photograph page 42). We
pass above the Quemada crater; Walk 3 circles it.

Shortly the route passes by Ye (where Walk 3 ends), a
small farming community cast across a sloping plateau
below Corona's gaping crater. Crossing the plateau, you
look straight down into deep valleys. In spring the top of

the plateau is flecked with poppies, dandelions, daisies and *Echium*. A porthole window set in a stone wall that encloses a carpark is all that gives away the **Mirador del Río ★** (📷). This well-camouflaged lookout is embedded in the top of the **Risco** (Cliff) **de Famara ★**. From here you look straight out over the Río channel onto the bare and barren — yet strangely beautiful — Graciosa Island, which sits just below. This is a view unequalled on Lanzarote, and one of the best vistas in all the Canaries. The mountain island (Montaña Clara) and Alegranza enhance this already magnificent sea view. The *mirador* balcony hangs out over a precipitous wall plummeting 450m/1475ft below, and you look down onto the landscapes of Walk 2 shown on pages 37 and 38: the exquisite Playa del Risco and the captivating salt pans of El Río Note: the exterior of this setting is worth seeing from the cliff-top above (from where the photograph on page 17 was taken). The *mirador* occupies the site of a 16th-century pirate lookout.

Continuing south, we edge along the cliffs of Famara. This wall of rock stretches for 23km and reaches a height of 600m/1970ft, as it slices its way along the northwest coast. The road (one-way, fortunately) is narrow and vertiginous — even on foot! You recapture the very dramatic *mirador* vista a little further on, where you are able to pull over safely. In the distance ahead you see the vast Jable plain stretching inland behind Playa de Famara, and the hills growing up out of the west coast.

Leaving the plateau we overlook a rocky basin of farmland — the other side of Ye. Pass the most stunning picnic spot on the island (**P**2) — also set in these cliffs. Meet a junction at 68km and continue straight on for Haría/Arrecife. Descending to **Máguez** (72km ✗ **P**3), we cross a large declining valley. See the

Car tours 1 and 2: The restaurant at Monumento al Campesino is a beautifully-restored farmhouse.

Montaña Corona, rising off the plateau behind Máguez (Picnic 3)

craters over on your right? Walk 3 (Alternative) circles this very quiet and scenic mound of volcanoes. Máguez is a rambling, pleasantly scruffy country village with a peaceful air about it. Keep right on entering the village ... or turn left for the picnic spot.

Over in the next valley lies **Haría** (74km ✕ M), a handsome settlement embellished with palms. This oasis of greenery boasts the largest number of palms in the Canaries. (I wonder what Gomera has to say about this?) Bougainvillea, geraniums, and hibiscus splash the village with colour, and the grand shady plaza adds a touch of class. Keep right through the narrow streets, to continue to Teguise. Exiting this valley of palms we wind up a rocky crest. Some 4km from Haría we pass the Mirador de Haría (📷✕). Just beyond the *mirador*, we head below Lanzarote's highest (but barely noticeable) summit — Las Peñas del Chache (670m/2200ft), which houses a miltary installation.

Car tour 2: The green lagoon that sits at the foot of the Golfo crater. Rich volcanic hues and an intense blue sea enhance this splendid setting. See also page 24.

Descending out of the hills we make a 3km side-trip, by turning up a road signposted for Las Nieves (on the right). *Note:* This is the *second* turn-off for Las Nieves that you come to. The Ermita de las Nieves (**P**4) stands in solitude, high on a windswept plateau. The 18th-century chapel (open only on the patron saint's day in September) marks the site where the Virgin appeared to a young shepherd. From the edge of the plateau you have a splendid view down onto the extensive Playa de Famara and over the semi-desert Jable plain. The Risco de Famara topples off to an abrupt end here.

Stone walls fence off the countryside on our approach to Los Valles. The interior of the island opens up, as low-slung valleys peel back and rounded hillocks rise in the background. **Los Valles** (88km) sits on the edge of a sweeping basin patched in huge cultivated squares. Here we find the best examples of the traditional Arcadian houses — low oblong buildings with very few (and very small) windows. Cocks (haystacks) set amidst the houses and farm buildings set off this rural landscape. Beyond Los Valles we cross the basin and bump our way into Teguise. Pass the turn-off to the 16th-century Castillo de Santa Bárbara (■;1.3km up a gravel road). This modest fortress commands a good view over the surrounding countryside from its volcano-edge perch. It was once a watchtower to warn against the raiding Moors.

Teguise★ (95km ✕✝✝M; drawing page 4), the island's ancient capital, is Lanzarote's showplace. The village still retains its original character of cobbled streets, stately old buildings, and spacious plazas. In the main square you'll find the imposing Church of San Miguel and, just off the square, the 18th-century Palacio de Spinola. The convents of Santo Domingo and San Francisco are hidden in amongst the houses.

Leaving the glaring whiteness of Teguise, follow the GC730 as far as the La Caleta/Famara turn-off, 3km out. Now we make for the coast. The dusty fishing village of **La Caleta de Famara** (112km ▲✕) boasts some fine seafood restaurants. To reach the quieter end of this long black-sand beach, pass through the bare *urbanización* and take the track below the cliffs.

Returning to the GC730, bear right and enter **Mozaga** (126km ✕⛽; see Tour 2). At the intersection here we turn left and head home via **San Bartolomé** (keep right through the village) and **Tías** — the outgoing route for Tour 2.

Car tour 2: Looking across the beach of El Golfo crater, from the lookout point just above the village of El Golfo. You can't see the lagoon from this point; it is illustrated on page 23.

2 TIMANFAYA AND THE SOUTHERN BEACHES

Puerto del Carmen • San Bartolomé • Tinajo • La Santa • Montañas del Fuego • Yaiza • El Golfo • Playa Blanca • Papagayo • Femés • La Geria Valley • San Bartolomé • Puerto del Carmen

150km/93mi; 4 hours driving (plus 1 hour's coach tour in the National Park); Exit B from Puerto del Carmen
En route: *P*6, 7, 8, 9; Walks 5, 6, 7, 8, 9

Roads are generally narrow, bumpy and slow going. Some 16km of road is gravel (at press date). Watch for pedestrians and animals on the roads; both are oblivious to traffic.

Opening hours:
Timanfaya National Park: 09.00-17.00 daily, with coach tours operating from 09.00-16.00 daily
Monumento al Campesino: 10.00-17.00 Mondays to Fridays; 10.00-19.00 Saturdays, Sundays and holidays

This southern route allows you plenty of time for short strolls, a swim, and perhaps some wine-tasting — if you make a day of it. Volcanology may not be one of your favourite topics, but this drive will certainly arouse your interest in it. Over the last two and one-half centuries violent eruptions have left a curious landscape in their wake. The National Park bus tour — a must for everyone — immerses you in this moonscape of rich volcanic hues. It will be the highlight of your day, if not of your entire holiday on Lanzarote. More curiosities follow, however. La Geria, the valley of ash, and the home of *malvasia* wine, is another amazing sight. Here the vineyards create a scenery of their own. The eroded Golfo crater, with its dazzling green lagoon, is something akin to an artist's palette, with all its colours and blended hues. And if all this isn't enough, then there are the golden sandy beaches of the southeast, of which Papagayo has become the most popular amongst tourists. You'll soon see why.

Leave Puerto del Carmen on the Tías (5km ✗🍴) road (Exit B, the return route of Tour 1). We bypass Tías, cross straight over the GC720, and wind up over hills into the vast sloping valley overlooked by **San Bartolomé** (11km ✗). Volcanic cones stand above us. Vivid splashes of scarlet poppies, white daisies, and yellow dandelions light up the surrounding farmlands. Head straight through this sprawling village, keep to the right of the main square and, when you reach the GC740, turn left for Tinajo.

At the junction for Mozaga (14km ✗🍴) we're confronted with another of Manrique's works — the Monumento al Campesino ★, dedicated to the island's country dwellers. This bold ultra-modern structure stands in pleasant surroundings, with a restaurant (a beautifully-restored farmhouse; see page 21) that specialises in local dishes, and a small souvenir shop. Passing through the junction, we come into the hamlet of **Mozaga**. The setting is particularly picturesque: the houses are dispersed amidst great blocks of lava, which are brightly speckled with green *Aeoniums*. Neat, fresh-green garden plots border the lava plain.

Tao (17km ✕🎦) occupies a slight rise with a fine view across the sweeping Jable plain to the cliffs of Famara and the islands. A sprinkling of elegant palms complements this pleasant rural setting. We pass through **Tiagua** (18km ✕) in the thick of these gardens.

An avenue of palms leads us into the expansive farming settlement of **Tinajo** (23km ✕🚍), where Walk 5 ends. Entering the village, turn right for La Santa. Descending to the coast, the red Montaña Bermeja catches your eye, rising off the shore below left. The countryside becomes harsher, rough and bumpy with hillocks, and the terrain is strewn with stones. **La Santa** (28km ✕) is a small village of restaurants set back off the shore. The rather exclusive sports complex, Club La Santa (30km ⛰️✕), lies a couple of kilometres further on. It overlooks the rocky islet, La Isleta, and a pretty lagoon. A pleasant interlude in this desolate stretch of coast. To cross the *isleta*, pass the hotel entrance and then keep right.

Returning to Tinajo, keep straight on through the village to **Mancha Blanca** (41km), where we turn off for Montañas del Fuego. Mancha Blanca, starting point for Walk 5, rests on a shelf overlooking its tidy ash fields, on the edge of a sea of lava that floods the southwest. Everything here grows in straight rows, as you can see in the photograph on page 49. The village is the home of the island's female patron saint — Our Lady of the Volcanoes, who is credited with having saved Tinajo from a lava flow. A popular festival celebrates the saint's day on September 15th each year.

When we mount the lava plateau another world awaits us: the world of fire and brimstone, where two centuries ago all hell let loose and (as one witness described it) "the earth suddenly opened up and an enormous mountain rose from the bosom of the earth and from its apex shot flames which continued to burn for 19 days". This catastrophic eruption lasted intermittently for some six years (1730 to 1736), burying one-third of the island (including eleven villages) under metres of lava … an eruption unsurpassed in recorded history. Less than one hundred years later another eruption increased the existing number of volcanoes from 26 to 29.

Crossing this lonely but curiously beautiful landscape is like being on another planet, hence it should come as no surprise to learn that the first astronauts were shown photographs of the national park in preparation for their moon flight. The road cuts its way through rough sharp lava. Lichen flecks the rock, creating the impression of freshly fallen sleet. An assortment of volcanoes with hints of red, clay brown, and deep maroon grow out of the lava.

Large mounds of cinder soon close in on us. Some 9km from Mancha Blanca we turn off for **Islote de Hilario**—the departure point for the coach tours ★. An entrance fee, which includes your coach tour, is paid as you go into the park area. Islote de Hilario is named for a hermit (Hilario) who returned here after the eruptions had subsided to build a hut and plant a fig tree (which, incidentally, is *not* the fig in the restaurant...) — the only tree in the national park. The restaurant here makes good use of the thermal energy — temperatures reaching 360°C only six metres below the surface of the ground. Your excursion bus twists up, down, and around the great volcanoes, affording you stunning views over the park and into the craters of the Montañas del Fuego, which drip with endless blends of colours (see page 19).

Leaving the park and continuing south, we climb and pass alongside the russet-brown slopes of Montaña del Fuego, where the much-publicised camel ride ★ begins (at 56km). You're bound to see a camel train ascending or descending — complete with awkwardly-seated tourists astride the hump-backs. Still, it's an impressive sight, no matter how 'touristic'. Also, take note of the different type of lava formation on the left-hand side of the road here: this lava, with great cracks in its crust, is *pahoehoe* lava (also known as 'ropey lava'; the name is Hawaiian).

Out of the lava fields we come into the charming white-washed village of **Yaiza** (61km ✕🍴⊕♁), where Walk 7 begins and ends. Turn right at the junction here. Pass the cool, shady Los Remedios Square. Across from it stands the 18th-century church of the same name. This proud village has some fine old balconied houses, and the gardens overflow with colour. Barely 2km from Yaiza we leave the main south road and fork off right onto a gravel road to make for El Golfo. A traffic island full of geraniums marks the intersection. Bouncing over potholes we re–enter more jagged lava fields; these are interrupted by stony *islotes* (islands of lava-free ground; see photograph page 47). Keep left at the fork just over 4km along.

Meet the road to El Golfo and bear right. Crossing a crest, you descend to **El Golfo** ★ (69km ✕⚞☎⚟), a small seaside village of restaurants. The encompassing dark lava is lit up by bushes of resplendent green *tabaiba*. An unmarked *mirador* just before the village gives you an excellent view (see page 24) over the eroded Golfo crater★. This majestic submarine volcano has been spectacularly eaten away by the sea, leaving one with the impression that it has been sliced in half. The best access to the *golfo*, the crescent-shaped bay, is 2km back along the road. The first fork-off right leads you to a large parking area. Strolling down to the crater, you're greeted by a striking sight: an array of greys, browns, and reds oozes out of the cone and surrounding rock. A strong blue sea and a cloudy green lagoon ★ set at the base of the crater enhance this rainbow of colours, shown on page 23.

Following the coastline further south, we drive through billowing waves of lava. The colourful Montaña Bermeja soon commands your attention with its glowing orange-brown cone. Less than 2km from El Golfo's crater, you'll come to an unsignposted lay-by on your right. From here a path leads off to a *mirador* called Los Hervideros (⚞☎⚟; the 'boiling springs'), where the sea pounds into sea-caves. There's little to see here. However, from another lay-by 200m further along, the sight is made more impressive because the bright cone of Montaña Bermeja stands in the background. The lazy hills of Los Ajaches, leaning one against the other, rise up prominently ahead. Las Breñas is the village you see sprinkled along a raised shelf at the foot of the hills.

Turning inland, we round the salt pans of Janubio (Las Salinas de Janubio; see photograph page 61). They lie cradled in a deep basin off a land-locked lagoon and the curving black sand beach of Janubio. You look down onto a fine mosaic of tiny white squares of drying salt and ponds. The colours of this basin turn the severe countryside into quite a beauty spot, especially in the evening. Entering the hamlet of **La Hoya** — and just before rejoining the main south road — an unsignposted lookout (⚞☎⚟) allows you to pull over and get a few photographs of this interesting sight — the setting for Walk 8.

Head right along the GC720 for Playa Blanca. Some 800m along, a crest jutting out above the lagoon (a signposted *mirador,* ☎) enables you to view the *salinas* from the other side. The turn-off for **Picnic 8** and the beach (signposted 'Playa') comes up after another 800m. Then, crossing the featureless, stone-strewn Rubicón plain, we reach **Playa Blanca** (98km ▲▲▲✕🏪 and ⛴ to Fuerteventura), a small fishing village swallowed up by a mass of bungalows, hotels, apartments and all the paraphernalia of tourism. Fuerteventura sits enticingly close — just a 40-minute ferry trip away.

The only reason that I would bring you this far south is to see the unspoilt beaches that hide in the scenic southeastern coastline. Once in Playa Blanca, bear left and remain on this road all the way out to Papagayo (6km away). On the outskirts of Playa Blanca, meet a T-junction and keep right along a gravel road. For the first few kilometres you may encounter roadworks. There is a plan to build a tarred road all the way out to Papagayo. There's no signposting at present, and tracks branch off in all directions to the various beaches en route. Stay on the main track/road, just by following everyone else. You'll cross a barren stony shelf that lies at the foot of the Ajaches hills. All the beaches along here are different, and all are enticing. Just choose amongst them! Before reaching Papagayo, we branch off left to Playa de Puerto Muelas (better known to tourists — and signposted — as 'La Caleta'). This is the unofficial — and, needless to say, very popular — nudist beach. **Papagayo**, with its few derelict houses, is the hippy hangout. All the other beaches are for you and me — perhaps for enjoying **Picnic 9** (photograph page 64).

Femés, our next destination, *can* be reached via a dusty gravel road that cuts across the Rubicón (had we taken the first or second turn-off right immediately outside of Playa Blanca). But it's more comfortable to go via Las Breñas. So we return to the junction for El Golfo and turn right. Keeping left through **Las Breñas**, meet a T-junction and ascend to the left. A superb panorama over the plain to Playa Blanca and out to Fuerteventura soon unfolds. You see the 'pimply' island of Lobos and the white dunes of Corralejo directly behind it. The hills tower above you, with ridges tumbling out of them in all directions. The road zig-zags up to a narrow pass, and just on the saddle sits **Femés** (118km ✕☎), overlooking the flat Rubicón plain. Your view is framed by the encircling hills. Take a break and enjoy the vista from this *mirador* — or **Picnic 7**. The church is dedicated to San Marcial, the island's patron saint. Femés is a precious little village, set high up in an already elevated valley and shut off from the rest of the island.

Exiting through fields, we drop down out of the valley and back onto the GC720. Cross straight over the main road and join the GC730 just above **Uga** (124km ✖). Uga is a colourful village with a North African flavour about it. It rests in a saucer of gardens with its back up against the dark lava sea of the Timanfaya National Park. Continue straight on at the junction above Uga. Rounding a corner, the scenery changes yet again, as we enter the intriguing valley of La Geria (**P**6, 600m past the junction), a dark sweeping depression, further pitted with hollows. The slopes are coated in black ash. Myriad low half-moon stone walls edge the hollows and stretch across the countryside (see photographs on pages 51 and 53). This is the home of *malvasia* wine, the product of an ingenious farming method: The vines are planted in crater-like depressions layered with *lapilli*, which absorb the moisture from the air and enable a single vine to produce up to as much as 200 kilos of grapes. (Note: the valley road is very narrow here — so hopefully you will not meet any oncoming traffic....)

Leaving La Geria, we re-enter the lava — this time 'ropey' lava, which still has molten lava flowing under its solidified surface. (The ripples and ruptures in the surface are caused by this movement.) Strips of encroaching 'AA' lava, encrusted with lichen, give the effect of stagnant, weed-infested ponds. Cheerful green *Aeoniums* freckle the landscape. **Masdache** (135km ✖) lies amidst this upheaval of lava. Here's your chance to do some wine-tasting, at the *bodega* on the outskirts of the village. But remember: you still have to drive home! A row of prominent, gaping craters lines the landscape on your right. Re-entering vineyards and vegetable gardens, serenity returns to the countryside. A couple of kilometres beyond Masdache, we turn off right for San Bartolomé where we rejoin this morning's route. Entering San Bartolomé, keep straight on until you reach an intersection where you will see an avenue of palm trees across from you. Here turn right and continue straight on past the village square, to return to your base at Puerto del Carmen.

1 AROUND LA GRACIOSA

Distance: 19km/11.8mi; 3h15min
Grade: easy, but fairly long. Can be very hot. No shade
Equipment: comfortable shoes, sunhat, light cardigan, raingear, swimwear, suncream, picnic, plenty of water
How to get there: 🚢 from Orzola to La Graciosa departs 10.00 daily; connecting 🚌 from Arrecife departs 08.00 daily
To return: 🚢 from La Graciosa departs 16.00 daily; connecting 🚌 from Orzola departs 17.00 daily

Short walk: from Caleta del Sebo to the tidal lagoon (45min; easy). Heading out from Caleta del Sebo turn off left for the cemetery (see map), which lies 10min up. Then descend to the sea, bearing slightly right. In 7min, you'll reach the lagoon . . . if the tide is in. This is a beautiful spot to spend the day if you don't want to walk far; the return along the seashore takes 25 minutes. Note that there's little shade.

All of you will have seen La Graciosa from the Mirador del Río. The vista is unsurpassed. For many people, this view from the mirador is sufficient. But this little desert island deserves a second chance. Take a ferry over and see for yourself. You'll discover superb beaches, sand dunes, lop-sided craters, and a lagoon. The fishing village, Caleta del Sebo, seems to be in perpetual slumber; a relaxing calm pervades. There are no roads, and thus no traffic. You'll follow tracks by Shanks's pony.

Getting there is fun in itself. Taking the pint-sized ferry over, you pass through the straights of El Río in the shadows of the towering Famara cliffs. (Note: the sea can be choppy!)

Once you've got your legs back on steady ground again — on the quay at Caleta del Sebo, **head off** along the waterfront to the left. The village is a simple fishing haven of small low-slung houses. There are no gardens, no trees. Stark naked! At the end of the promenade, veer inland up past Bar Girasol Playa (which is also a pension). A dusty track takes you up onto a gravel road on your right. Remain on this road.

Out of the houses you cross a sandy/gravelly flat area, covered in various species of salt-resistant vegetation — *Launaea arborescens* (aulaga), *Mesembryanthemum nodiflorum* (cosco), *barilla* (the 'ice plant'), *Schizogyne sericea* and *Traganum moquinii*. Looking back down the track you have a superb shot over the village clustered along the water's edge to the dramatic Risco de Famara and the striking Playa del Risco (Walk 2), curving round the foot of the cliffs. On windy days you'll curse this dusty terrain. The two volcanoes, Pedro Barba (right) and Montaña del Mojón (left), rise up ahead on either side of the track. A third, Montaña Clara (an island), soon appears in the background, centred between the other two.

Three minutes past a branch to the left the track forks, just in front of the village dump. Go right for Caleta de Pedro Barba. Reddish *cosco* brightens up the inclines. Heading along the base of Montaña Pedro Barba, your view stretches beyond the wall of cliffs to the Jable plain and the distant volcanoes of Timanfaya. Some **40min** from the village cross a low crest and descend onto a lower plain, edged by short, abrupt hills. Alegranza comes into sight, rising up out of the sea into an impressive table-topped mountain trailed by a tail of hills. The remains of rock walls come as a surprise out here. What could they have grown?

At just over **50min** come to a branch-off left — our continuation, which circles the island. But why not first visit the beautifully-kept little port of Caleta de Pedro Barba: stay on the main track and head to the right; it's only seven minutes away. All the fishermen's old cottages there have been given glamorous 'facelifts'. Gardens filled with palms and shrubs encircle them, and a sandy cove sits just below. The good-sized jetty, which encloses a pool, points to the fact that this is no ordinary weekend retreat — it's a lovely serene spot with a good outlook over the cliffs and to Orzola.

Continuing around the island, we head towards Alegranza on a rougher track. The north coast is sandier; dunes grow into the landscape. Ignore the faint forks off to the right within the next ten minutes. *Polycarpaea nivea*, a dense, silvery-leafed plant, grows in the dunes. *Suaeda vera* crowns the little ant hills of sand that cover the plain. Montaña Bermeja (Red Mountain) soon appears on your left, and Montaña Clara reappears, seemingly joined to the island. At about **1h20min** the track forks; keep left and head towards the dunes to make for Playa del Ambar. What appears at first to be a lovely beach soon becomes a disappointment — it's littered with washed-up rubbish. Moreover, the rocks beneath the water's surface make swimming here awkward. The setting, however, makes an appealing photograph — the white dunes, green sea, and the volcanic-coloured mountains in the background. Don't worry — a better beach is en route! *Note:* the west-coast beaches are usually treacherous; take care when swimming!

The track heads around behind and above the beach, fading as it crosses the dunes. Just after dropping down to

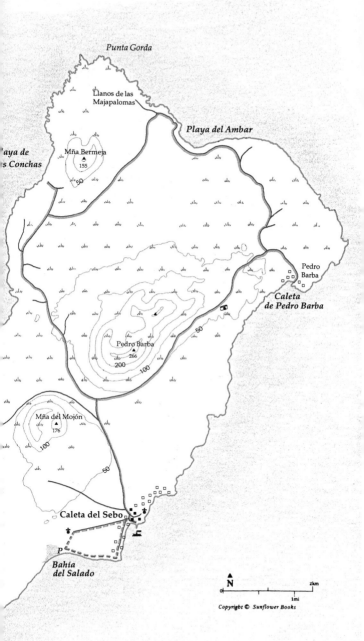

Punta Gorda

Llanos de las
Majapalomas

Playa del Ambar

Playa de
s Conchas

Mña Bermeja
▲
155

50

Pedro
Barba

Caleta
de Pedro Barba

50

Pedro Barba
▲ 266
200

100

Mña del Mojón
▲
176

100

50

Caleta del Sebo

P

Bahía
del Salado

N

0 ——————— 2km
————————————
1mi

Copyright © Sunflower Books

Playa de las Conchas, at the foot of Montaña Bermeja

the shoreline, a few minutes around the beach, we mee
our turn-off, some 30min from the Caleta de Pedro Barba
junction. Attention: it's a very faint track striking off left; i
quickly becomes more obvious. Don't continue straigh
on; that way leads to Punta Gorda.

Shortly you're alongside Montaña Bermeja. The dunes
lose their strength and flatten out, and Pedro Barba now reveals its crater. Further along, the Timanfaya side o
Lanzarote comes into sight. Approaching the coas
(**2h05min**), you come to a T-junction (just before a strip o
sand dunes). Now an exquisite beach lies only ten
minutes along to your right. It rests at the foot of the deep
maroon slopes of Montaña Bermeja. This clean beach o
golden sands, Playa de las Conchas (see above) drop:
deeply into a blue sea. Montaña Clara stands up boldly,
across the water. This is a prize spot . . . but don't forget to
check: how are you doing for time?

A left turn at the T-junction (2h05min) takes yo
between the two craters and back to Caleta del Sebo. It's a
gentle ascent over a low col littered with stones and rocks
Ignore all the branch-offs. Heading between the crater:
the Risco reappears like a green stage curtain, bringing ar
end to the walk. At **2h50min** you rejoin the track on whic
you started out; turn right for the port. All the boa
passengers congregate around the Marinero bar
restaurant before the boat leaves. So grab yourself a much
deserved cool beer. You'll spot the bar as you re-enter the
village: pass the Pension Enriqueta and turn left.

2 RISCO DE FAMARA

Map page 40; another photograph page 17
Distance: 13.5km/8.3mi; 3h

Grade: very strenuous — a steep, gravelly descent down a cliff face, with a **possibility of vertigo** for inexperienced walkers. The return is a tough ascent of 400m/1315ft — sheer slog! Don't attempt in wet weather. There's no shade en route, so the walk is not advisable on *very* hot days. Only recommended for experienced and fit walkers.

Equipment: walking boots, sunhat, light jacket, raingear, swimwear, suncream, picnic, plenty of water

How to get there: 🚌 to Ye (departs Arrecife) or Máguez (and walk to the starting point; add 45min), or alight at Haría and take a taxi. *To return:* 🚌 from Máguez

This is a truly spectacular walk. You descend into the landscape viewed from the Mirador del Río and slip and slide your way down the sheer Risco (cliff) de Famara. You discover that the captivating beach that sits imbedded in the lava tongue hundreds of metres below you is accessible after all! (The local people will probably hang me when they find out I've revealed this little-known beauty spot to you....) In the early morning and in the evening, this setting is no less than an oil painting. You'll probably want to make this an all-day hike, so *do* be prepared for the lack of shade.

Alight from the Ye bus at the Mirador del Río junction just before Ye. The road here, to your left (descending from the *mirador*) is for south-bound traffic only. **Setting out** by heading up this road, we pass through the outskirts of Ye. The houses are shuttered and many of the plots lie in tired abandon. Low lichen-clad stone walls criss-cross a countryside clothed in fig trees and prickly pear.

Our first turn-off comes up at **5min.** Landmarks: Soon after a roadside house on your right, you'll see a dyke (natural wall of rock) with a stone wall built into it. It's on the left. Two stone buildings, leaning up against the road, stand behind it. Follow the track that turns off immediately before this wall. A stunning panorama slowly unravels, as you near the cliff-tops a few minutes along. You look straight out on to the stark sandy island of Graciosa (Walk 1), bare of vegetation, desolate, and yet quite beautiful in the eyes of many beholders.... The fishing village of Caleta del Sebo nestles around the exposed shoreline, its small white houses staring up at you. Montaña Clara is the blade of rock that bursts up out of the sea behind La Graciosa and, further afield, to the right, lies the hilly island of Alegranza.

When the track ends continue straight on, now

35

descending on a rocky path. Standing on the very edge of the cliff, you look along a sheer wall of rock that plummets to a flat shelf below. Playa del Risco steals your attention with its golden sand and shallow turquoise-green water. Another sight distracts you: the strangely-coloured pink and maroon (and sometimes orange) ponds of the abandoned salt pans of the Salinas del Río.

One wonders where the path goes from here! It swings down to the right of the power pylon. The view is captivating to say the least; however this path *requires your utmost attention!* No stretches of it are really vertiginous, but you zig-zag straight down. All forks rejoin, so don't worry about deviations. An astonishing amount of plant life clings to these cliffs (see photograph page 17), which harbour the richest source of plant life on Lanzarote. A number of very rare species, as well as nearly all the island's endemic plants are found in this northern massif. In and around these *riscos* you can find *Pulicaria canariensis, Asteriscus schultzii, Reichardia, Kickxia, Aichryson tortuosum,* two species of *Aeonium, Limoniums,* the rare *Echium decaisnei,* a yellow-flowering *Argyranthemum,* and many different grasses.

The desert-like Jable plain and the assortment of volcanic cones that constitute the Timanfaya National Park soon become visible over to the left. Approaching the faint track that cuts across the sea-flat below, you meet a fork. The right-hand branch is clearer, and in thirty minutes from the top of the cliff it takes you to the track. Turn right along it. Looking back up the way you came, you're bound to be impressed. Moreover, you know that at least here you *can* escape the press of tourists…. Five minutes along, clamber across a dry, gouged-out stream-bed and, five minutes later, the track passes through a stone wall. Some 100m/yds before the wall, you'll spot a faint path descending the side of the bank to reach the beach (**50min**).

Nirvana! At last you can fling off your clothes (hoping that the periscope at the Mirador del Río isn't trained on you …) and plunge into the cool sea. *Note:* Watch out for broken glass on the beach. Now, whether you decide to swim first or explore the salt pans, your continuation is along this lovely stretch of beach. La Graciosa is just across the straight — almost within swimming distance. At the end of the beach, scramble over the stones and rejoin your track, following it to its end (by an electricity transformer station). The cliffs stand before you — a

The Salinas del Río are one of Lanzarote's undiscovered — and not easily accessible — sights. See also page 38.

formidable barrier of rock. See if you can locate the *mirador* in the cliffs above: this will show you just how well it fits in with its surroundings.

From the track make your way over to the salt pans, again watching out for broken glass. Pass the remains of a derelict building. Towards the end of the pans (*salinas*) you come to the second 'sight' of the walk: a magnificent pink, milk-of-magnesia-coloured pond enclosed by crumbling stone walls (see above). On a fine day you have a clear reflection of the *Risco* in it. On occasions the pools of the shallower pond reached before this one glow a brilliant orange (see page 38).

We return by crossing a footwalk that circles the pink ponds, cutting across the salt pan. Rejoin the track some ten minutes back, then keep left along it. When it fades out a few minutes on, veer uphill to your left — you'll find it becomes clear again. Turn right at a T-junction and remain on the track until your ascending point, barely fifteen minutes along. Relocating the return path requires a keen eye. Four minutes beyond the gouged-out streambed and 100m/yds past a small watercourse (which you cross), you'll see a small pile of stones on your left, marking the ascending point. The ascent is now straightforward. A little over thirty minutes off the track you reach the power pylon. From here we head south on an old path that hugs the edge of the cliff, and we can take in the last of this memorable view. (This stretch of path might prove unnerving for some walkers.) You scale the side of a ridge running parallel to the old washed-out route to the salt pans. Soon come on to a track; follow it up over the crest. Remain on the main track, ignoring all branch-offs.

Descending now, two craters — one stepped above the other — dominate the Guinate Valley below you. The village of Guinate occupies a quiet cultivated corner. Around twenty minutes from the power pylon you exit onto the main road and descend to Máguez (right). The *plaza*/bus stop lies twenty-five minutes downhill.

The Salinas del Río

3 MAGUEZ • CASAS LA BREÑA • YE

Distance: 9.5km/6mi; 1h45min

Grade: moderate, with a steady 30-minute climb at the end of the walk. Can be cold and misty.

Equipment: comfortable shoes, jacket, sunhat, raingear, suncream, picnic, plenty of water

How to get there: 🚌 to Máguez (departs from Arrecife)
To return: 🚌 from Ye (*reconfirm departure time before setting out!*), or walk back to Máguez for the bus (add 1h), or telephone the Haría taxi (tel: 83 50 31).

Alternative walk: Máguez—Guinate—Máguez (1h40min; fairly strenuous — with a steep 45-minute ascent at the start — but short). Head straight uphill from the bus stop, following the Mirador del Río sign. Five minutes up, just beyond the second junction, fork off left up a narrow lane into the houses. Metres up the way becomes a track. You remain on this track all the way to Guinate, where the track ends — 100m/yds up from the main north road. A turn-off to the right, some 20min into the walk, heads over into a crater (the site of a small tip) four minutes away. The crater walls harbour an interesting collection of flora. From the top of the plateau, midway along the walk, you have a magnificent view out over the islands. When you reach the main road, bear right for Máguez, 20min away. The bus leaves from the village plaza at the intersection.

On this pleasant countryside ramble we wind our way amidst the hills of the Famara massif — the highest and (in winter) the most lush corner of the island. Farm plots keep us company. Masses of solid stone walls fortify the inclines. In spring the herbaceous slopes are flecked with dandelions, indigo *Echium*, gold-coloured *Asteriscus*, white *Argyranthemum*, and mauve and scarlet poppies. A splendid sight! The massive yawning craters of Montaña Corona and La Quemada, and the neighbouring Malpais (badlands) de la Corona remind us of the volcanic origins of Lanzarote.

Our walk begins at the small plaza where the bus stops, at an intersection. Follow the road diagonally across from you, the one that heads straight into the village. A minute along pass the colourful church square. Two minutes later, just beyond a large garden plot, we reach an intersection. Turn up left. Ascending (keep straight up) you look back over the village, spread along a gentle valley sprinkled with palms. Just over **5min** up, a road joins you from the right. A minute later, branch off right onto a farm track lined with palms. You exit through hills into another valley. Keep left at the fork a few minutes along, crossing a saucer-shaped valley dominated by the enormous crater of Montaña Corona (609m/1995ft; photograph page 22). A rough patchwork of cultivated fields stretches across the sloping inclines. Just over **20min** from

Máguez) we cross an intersection, and then pass two tracks forking off right. Rounding Montaña Corona, the palacial villa, Torrecilla de Domingo (see page 42), captures our attention. It sits high atop a ridge overlooking the northeastern inclines and the sea. On the slopes of Corona you see a plethora of colourful vegetation. But all colour drains out of the landscape, as we approach ash-covered fields and a vast labyrinth of stone walls. Off the hillside, we pass a branch-off to the right and enter this labyrinth.

Close to the Mirador del Río road, at around **40min** into the walk, the track forks. Bear left. On reaching the road, bear left again. A gap in the crater walls above gives you a good view of its sharp-toothed crown and an uninterrupted vista over the spiky interior of Malpaís de la Corona. Five minutes up the road a wide mule track flanked by high stone walls veers off to your right and descends towards the *malpais*. A track curves round in front of you five minutes later. Follow it downhill. Our route now circles another extinct volcano (La Quemada), which soon reveals a quite substantial crater. Looking back up the hillside you get a dramatic shot of Montaña Corona: its razor-sharp rim rears up above the wall-rutted slopes.

At **1h05min** exit onto the Orzola road. Turning left along the road, we continue along the edge of the *mal-*

Fig

pais. Some five minutes down the road, turn off onto a track that climbs steeply to your left, circling La Quemada. A steady — and, in stretches, steep — climb takes us up to Ye. Pass a branch-off left. You sidle up against the mountain and get a glimpse of the inside of the crater.

A little over fifteen minutes off the road come to a junction. Keep straight on — right. A deep valley slicing back into the plateau comes out of hiding. Our route dips down and crosses it. Ignore the smaller side tracks. At **1h30min** we ascend into another, higher valley, just below the plateau and come into Ye. This small village sits with its back to the gaping crater of Montaña Corona. Cross the road (to the Mirador del Río) and pick up the road heading into the village centre, to your right. The bus stop lies a couple of minutes along, just beside the public phone box.

The palacial villa of Torrecilla de Domingo against the backdrop of Montaña Corona (Car tour 1; Walk 3)

4 MALA • PRESA DE MALA • ERMITA DE LAS NIEVES • TEGUISE

Distance: 18.5km/11.5mi; 3h

Grade: quite strenuous, with a drawn-out ascent of 608m/1995ft lasting 1h45min. Can be quite cold, windy and misty ... or even wet!

Equipment: comfortable shoes, warm jacket, sunhat, raingear, suncream, picnic, plenty of water

How to get there: Máguez-🚌 to Mala (departs Arrecife)
To return: 🚌 from Teguise

Short walks: both are easy. Take private transport to start out; return by bus.
1 Ermita de las Nieves to Teguise (1h10min). Pick up the main walk at the chapel (Ermita de las Nieves) and follow it to the end.
2 Ermita de las Nieves to Mala (1h50min). Again, pick up the main walk at the chapel. Use the map to do the first half of the main walk in reverse; it's very straightforward — but see above notes on weather conditions.

Crossing the island from east to west, we climb to the solitary Chapel of the Snows (Ermita de las Nieves) — the coldest point on Lanzarote. So if you're after some bracing air ... join us and leave the sea plain! We wind up into a narrow concealed valley. The denuded clay-brown slopes soon fold up into pasture-like inclines (in winter). Seascapes and mountain views accompany us all the way up to the chapel — where from a windswept plateau we enjoy a 360° panorama — the view of views.

When you leave the bus at Mala (at the *second* stop, beside a telephone cabin), **start by** heading north along the road. Three minutes along, turn off up a road branching off left — the second one you come to, just past a line of palms and mimosas. Immediately in, the road forks. Bear right. Pass the church two minutes up. The village is immersed in fields of prickly pear. You can see the wall of the Presa (reservoir) de Mala ahead, wedged across the mouth of the Valle del Palomo.

Less than **10min** along come to an intersection. The road swings left; we continue straight ahead on a rough track. Our climb begins as we leave the farmland behind. Just before crossing the crest into the Valle del Palomo, we get a good view along the sea plain of Mala, buried under a dark green cloak of prickly pear, and then the carpet of tightly-woven gardens extending back to Guatiza. Close on **20min** up, pass a fork off to the right (to an abandoned building). To see the fish pond-sized reservoir— the only one on Lanzarote —, leave the track and cross the top of the crest; it's only two minutes over the top.

At the **40min**-mark we pass behind some houses and continue climbing. We cross the bed of the stream, and

43

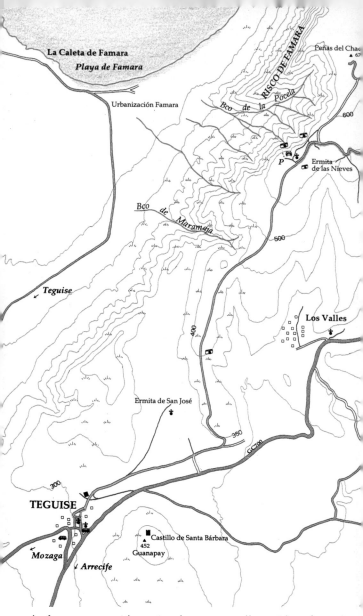

before us see a luxuriantly green valley. After the rains have fallen, this is the most luxuriant valley on Lanzarote. We recross the bed of the *barranco* and the track lazily zig-zags up out of the valley. Yellow, violet and scarlet flowers set the hillside alight. Catch a corner of Malpais de la Corona (Walk 3) over the hills. Mounting the plateau, you swing up past a Lilliputian farm dwelling leaning against a rocky nodule. Two dogs, 'Black' and 'White'(I've so christened them), will come tearing out — barking

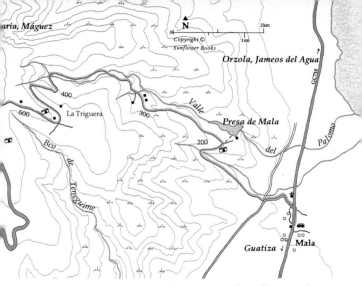

furiously. When they're ten feet away, they'll wag their tails and then jump all over you. Black and White keep you company until you reach the main road.

A minute beyond the farmhouse you circle an uninhabited house, and looking back, you have a fine view down onto Arrieta and the sea. To the northwest you see the plateau of Guatifay and the prominent cones of Corona and La Quemada. The great gap separating us from these craters is created by the valleys of Máguez and Haría — an impressive sight. Approaching **1h30min** you exit onto the GC700, bid farewell to Black and White, and head along to your left. Over to the right rises the island's highest summit, Las Peñas del Chache, crowned by a large military installation. As you descend, Llanos de Zonzamos (the sweeping plain behind Arrecife) comes into view, with Arrecife in the background. The refuge of Las Nieves soon captures your attention. It stands conspicuously alone on the *mesa*. Within ten minutes you reach the signposted turn-off to it. Los Valles is visible through the mouth of the *barranco* below. Soon the roar of the sea is heard, and a roadside *mirador* gives you a view over the Playa de Famara far below.

At **1h50min** you're alongside the chapel and probably getting a good battering from the wind. If this is the case, picnic inside the walls that enclose this peaceful haven. For an unparalleled vista head over the cliffs (*carefully*). Below you lies the beach of Famara and, beyond it, the desert-like Jable plain fans inland, littered with remnants of volcanoes. On our right, the Risco de Famara (Walk 2) ends abruptly in a razor-sharp tail; beyond lie the islands of La Graciosa (Walk 1), Montaña Clara and Alegranza.

Once you've soaked up this great view, continue out on the gravel road that descends south of the chapel. It follows the crest of this declining ridge towards Teguise. The local people use this road, and the odd tourist or two will bounce past in a jeep. Shortly the modest Castillo de Santa Bárbara becomes a prominent landmark. Fastened to the crater rim of Montaña Guanapay, it stands guard over Teguise and the encompassing plains. Heading back into fields you descend to an intersection, just over **2h35min** en route (having passed a track joining from the left beforehand). Here the main track turns left to join the GC700; however we keep straight on through the intersection. Ten minutes beyond the intersection, come to a wide track. Bear left along it.

Entering the rear of Teguise, pass the stadium and join a confusion of tracks. Keep straight on, aiming for the church tower. A street leads you down through houses and over a small bridge. Immediately beyond it, leave the street and cross an open space to the church. An arched portal lets you through into a pretty plaza. Exit alongside the Caja de Canarias. Take a peep inside this excellently-restored building. You come out to another beautiful square; here, outside a second church, catch your bus.

The Lilliputian dwelling where 'Black' and 'White' live. We've zig-zagged up out of the Valle del Palomo and now overlook Arrieta and the sea (1h30min into the walk).

5 MANCHA BLANCA • PLAYA DE LA MADERA • TINAJO

Distance: 25.5km/15-3/4mi; 3h30min

Grade: easy but long. Since there is no shade en route, this walk is not recommended in very hot weather. *Note also:* If you plan to swim in the rock pools or at the beach, make *absolutely certain* that the sea is safe. I have never swum at the beach myself, because it never looked safe enough to me!

Equipment: comfortable shoes, cardigan, sunhat, raingear, suncream, swimwear, picnic, plenty of water

How to get there: Tinajo-🚐 to Mancha Blanca (departs from Arrecife)
To return: 🚐 from Tinajo (or taxi)

This walk will not appeal to everyone. It takes you straight through the vast lava flows that have buried much of the southwest of Lanzarote. Not a soul lives out here — not even plants survive. It's a no-man's land. Deep in its midst, you stumble upon sunken islands of stony lava-free ground, called *islotes* (see below). Here you'll find some plant life and cultivation taking refuge. It's a curious landscape that few would dare to call beautiful, but it has a special allure.

Alight from your bus in Mancha Blanca at the Yaiza— Montaña del Fuego junction, and **set off** for Montaña del Fuego. Keep right when the road forks a minute downhill. We skirt this well-dispersed rural village. Stone walls hedge in the road and cordon off the countryside. Here we're on the edge of a sea of 'AA' lava (a sharp, unevenly-surfaced lava; see also Walk 3). The grand crater which dominates the scene is Montaña Blanca (see page 49), and a pint-sized off-sider sits in front of it.

Islotes — tiny oases of greenery (chiefly tabaiba) — light up the dark and inhospitable lava landscape that we explore on Walk 5.

At the T-junction less than **10min** along, head right. From here we follow tarred country lanes through fields. Five minutes later, head left (at the first turn-off). The sharp colour contrast of vivid green plots and ash-grey *lapilli* enhances this picturesque countryside. Montaña de Tenezar rises up boldly at the end of the road. Another junction awaits you at the foot of the mountain, **35min** into the walk. Turn left and continue on a gravel road. You head into lava that now takes over the landscape. Pass two forks off to the right. The craters of Montaña Blanca and son soon bulge up out of the lava. Up close, the mountain's rocky exterior resembles a freshly-baked cake.

Slowly, the off-shore islands appear: Alegranza, the furthest afield, Montaña Clara, and finally La Graciosa (Walk 1). The dark lava drops off into a deep blue sea. Without warning, suddenly the lava flow subsides and reveals a basin of low stony hillocks that lean up against Montaña Blanca like cushions. A couple of stone *casitas* can be seen, set in a coomb in the shoulders of the crater. This is Casas del Islote. We pass the fork-off left to Casas del Islote and Montaña del Fuego at about **1h10min** and dip down into an *islote*.

Some fifteen minutes further on pass another turn-off to the right. From a rise five minutes further on, you spot the first of the beaches, Playa de las Malvas. These black sand beaches are small and the waters usually turbulent. A tiny lagoon sits back off the beach here. Beyond this *playa* we head back into the lava again and, less than ten minutes

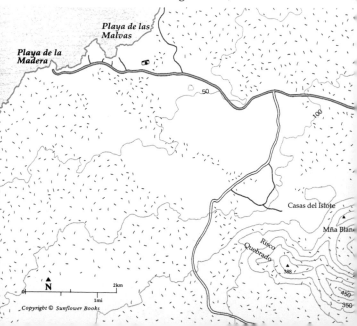

Playa de las Malvas

Playa de la Madera

50

100

Casas del Islote

Mña Blanc

Risco Quebrado

388

450

350

N

0

2km

1mi

The dark picon-covered gardens of Mancha Blanca, with the yawning crater of Montaña Blanca in the background (Car tour 2, Walk 5)

later, we drop down onto Playa de la Madera. This small cove doesn't look too friendly either. Play it safe and stick to the rock pools. Pillows of yellow-tipped *Zygophyllum fontanesii* (*uvilla* — 'little grapes') grow out of the sand. A path crosses the beach and climbs into the rock on the other side, where stone-built shelters provide good wind-breaks. Shallow and inviting rock pools (*only safe when the sea is calm*) lie beyond the shelters.

Some 1h10min into the straightforward return walk you rejoin the road at the Tinajo—Mancha Blanca junction. This time, keep straight on for Tinajo. La Graciosa is at last in full view, and the Risco de Famara (Walk 2) dramatises the landscape as it bursts straight up out of the sea. Tinajo is a sprinkling of hamlets that sprawls over a large cultivated plain. Entering the village, keep straight along (to the left), passing all turn-offs to the right. On reaching a large intersection, bear left, taking the second of the two roads leading down to the plaza, 1h40min from the beach (**3h30min**). The bus leaves from outside the *dulcería* (cake shop), across from the plaza.

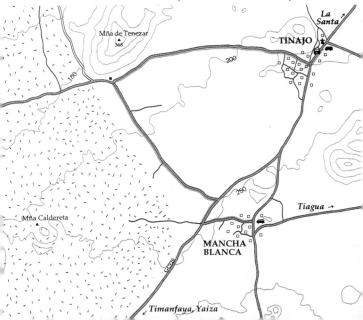

6 UGA • MONTAÑA GUARDILAMA • LA MONTAÑETA • MACHER • PUERTO DEL CARMEN

Distance: 12.5km/7.8mi; 2h15min

Grade: relatively easy, if the mountain ascent is excluded. The ascent of Guardilama involves a steep climb of 160m/525ft, sometimes over loose stones. Be careful on the descent. The climb is also to be avoided in hot weather, but remember, too, that the peak can be very cold and windy!

Equipment: walking boots, jacket, sunhat, suncream, raingear, picnic, plenty of water

How to get there: Playa Blanca- 🚌 to Uga (departures from Arrecife and Puerto del Carmen)
To return: 🚌 from Puerto del Carmen

Short walk: Simply exclude the mountain ascent; this takes 25 minutes off the total time and makes for an easy hike. Comfortable shoes are sufficient.

The island's farming methods are of much interest on Lanzarote. With great ingenuity the islanders have been able to grow a variety of produce. This hike takes you through the dark ash fields of La Geria — an intriguing landscape patterned by hollows and stone walls. You then cross the grassy summits that divide east and west, two quite different worlds! Here you'll see the wonders the country folk have worked with the land, and if you speak a little Spanish, they'll be only too proud to show you the way they've gone about it. The *mirador* atop Montaña Guardilama shows you a world of vivid contrasts: vineyards and vegetable plots, meadows and ash fields and the great lava flows. It opens up the interior of the island for you, and you have a fine outlook over the lunar landscape of the Timanfaya National Park.

Leave the bus outside the church in Uga. **Start out** from the bright and cheerful square here, by heading back the way you came in. Pass a restaurant and come to a junction. Swinging up left, you reach another junction a minute along. Here head left, above garden plots. Two minutes along leave the road and climb a farm track, the first one you come to. You strike off to the right. The route overlooks the village, which nestles in a shallow depression of gardens, its back to a vast expanse of crusty lava. Out of the lava rise the great fire mountains of Timanfaya, their inclines splashed with rust browns and reds. A cluster of adjoining hills stands to the south of the village. These climb into the southern massif — Los Ajaches.

The track carries us up to the Teguise road. A couple of minutes along it, to the left, we fork off right onto another

track heading into the hills above. We're now entering the
Geria Valley. Vines and fig trees fill the small hollows. The
ash fields are ornamented by an assortment of stone walls.
Our route takes us straight over the *cumbre*, the island's
spine. Ignore all turn-offs. Wandering through this
blackened world is quite extraordinary. Over to the left,

*From the summit of Montaña Guardilama, we look across the Geria
Valley to the volcanoes of Timanfaya. Myriad 'half-moon' stone walls
protect grape vines in the crater below (see also page 53).*

the lava fields grow into a vast lake ruptured by weather-worn cones, and above you stands a line of grass-capped hills that glow with greenery. The solitary white farmsteads stand out like sanctuaries in this inhospitable landscape. Before long, walls take over the countryside. You're entering the vineyards, and the inclines are pock-marked with depressions that are collared by half-circles of stone walls (see page 51 and opposite). We're in malmsey territory, where the well-known *malvasía* origi-nates. This myriad of walls could be the ruins of a grand ancient city.

Crossing the saddle of the *cumbre* the way eases out. You'll have a superb view back over La Geria and Timanfaya. Just over the pass, we turn off for the ascent of Montaña Guardilama, at **40min** into the walk. We follow a faint track that cuts off to the left a few metres beyond the last vineyard (some 150m/yds beyond the second branch-off to the right). Cross a grassy field, briefly running alongside the vineyards, then head straight up the mountain in front of you. When the track ends, continue straight up to the summit — a tiring climb, as it's *very* steep. Nearing the end of the climb, you're scrambling over loose rocks and stones, and this makes the descent quite difficult; *take care!* At the **55min**-mark you flop down on the summit. If it's a windy day, you won't be able to stand upright or even take photos up here! The panorama is, however, magnificent and encompasses the waves of hills in the south, as well as the Risco de Famara and La Graciosa and its neighbouring islets in the north. The sharp rocky crest drops straight down into a cultivated

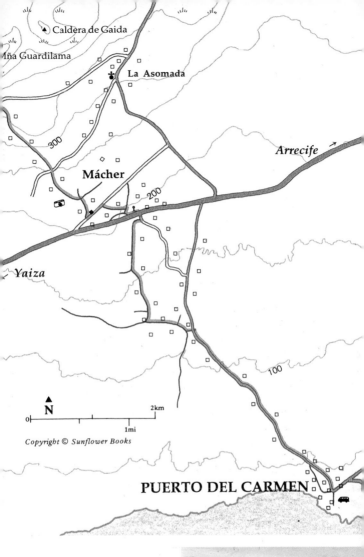

crater and out onto the pitted ash fields of La Geria (see photograph page 51). Uga and Yaiza lie to the southeast.

Descend slowly and carefully to the main track, where we bear left towards La Asomada. Three minutes along, we fork off the main

A closer view of the half-moon walls protecting malvasia vines in La Geria Valley (see also page 51).

track and descend another to the right. Dropping through plots, come to an intersection (within 10 minutes) and head straight through it. Pass two turn-offs left and, two minutes later, exit onto a road (**1h25min**). Notice the charming old house at the corner here.

Continue up the road to the left, and in two minutes branch off on a small track that heads down to the GC720 just below. When you reach it, cross it and, one minute along to the left, turn off onto a narrow road striking off right. A well-preserved windmill stands above the main road here. Immediately into the turn-off, veer right onto a track. Remain on this track for the next ten minutes, keeping straight down. At the T-junction at the bottom of the track bear left. Five minutes later, just after rounding a corner, you branch left again (the second left), to join the Puerto del Carmen road. The town lies 20 minutes downhill. If you're Arrecife-bound, keep left at the intersection inside the town, and one minute up find your bus stop.

Montaña Guardilama, seen from where our ascent begins. In springtime the slopes are speckled with wild flowers. Enjoy Picnic 6 at the foot of this inviting mountain, or make the steep climb, to enjoy the views shown on page 51.

Distance: 10km/6.2mi; 2h45min

Grade: fairly strenuous, with a steady 425m/1435ft ascent. Can be cold and windy.

Equipment: comfortable shoes, jacket, sunhat, raingear, suncream, picnic, plenty of water

How to get there: Playa Blanca-🚌 to Yaiza (departures from Arrecife and Puerto del Carmen)

To return: 🚌 from Yaiza

Short walk: Femés—Atalaya de Femés—Femés (1h; a strenuous, but short, ascent). Accessible by private transport only.

The view from the Atalaya de Femés is best appreciated at sunrise and sunset, when the shadows creep across the countryside, and the last (or first) light captures the real beauty of both Timanfaya and the Salinas de Janubio. Sitting high above the picturesque hamlet of Femés, you have the southern vista of Lanzarote all to yourself. On your ascent you'll often see camels grazing in one of the adjoining valleys. Nearer the summit, goats and a few sheep keep you company.

The bus drops you just before the square. The bleached-white village of Yaiza has won a number of awards for its appearance. It really is picture postcard-perfect, with its resplendent *bougainvillea* and graceful palms. We **start off** by taking the road that turns off left and heads up between the church and the square to a large parking area (from where it continues on to La Degollada). A couple of minutes out we come to a junction. Take the track off to the left, cutting across the valley floor. You look up into a tapering valley and see the hamlet of La Degollada ensconced at the end of it. Halfway across the valley floor you pass through an intersection and continue on a farm track. Ascending the valley wall, pass a faint fork-off left. Mount the crest just over **15min** from Yaiza. A track joins from the left; we continue up this plump ridge, which carries us all the way to the Atalaya de Femés. In the valley over on your left you may see camels.

As you climb, the island opens up, revealing a variety of scenery. Yaiza is in full view below, its brightness accentuated by the intense green garden plots and the dark sea of lava. A barrier of volcanoes, one running onto the next, fills in the backdrop. The track divides, both forks briefly running parallel — keep to the right-hand fork. Come to a fork just over five minutes up the ridge and bear right. Your view becomes more expansive and more rewarding — dipping down now onto Uga and stretching all the way up the dark, shadowy Geria Valley (Walk 6).

At about **30min** the track forks off into three different directions. Yours is the furthest to the right. Mounting another step in the ridge, we see over the sloping plains of the east to Puerto del Carmen and Arrecife. Looking north, notice the line of three lopsided craters. The way dips briefly before reascending, and you're given an introductory glimpse of the Femés Valley. Montaña de Timanfaya, the king of the volcanoes, dominates the National Park, with its distinct reddish-brown slopes.

The way fades as it remounts the top of the crest, which in turn narrows into a sheer-sided 'neck'. Another striking sight follows: the off-white salt pans and the khaki-green lagoon of the Salinas del Janubio shimmering in the sun. Scaling the final head of hills, the track briefly disappears,

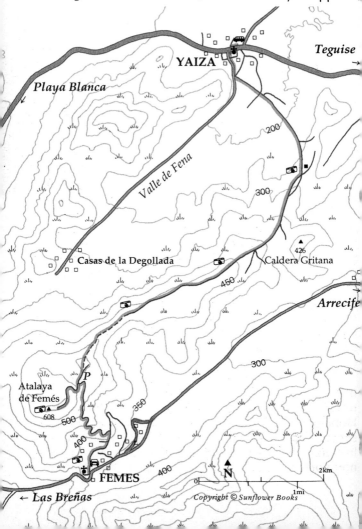

On the climb to the Atalaya de Femés we overlook La Degollada, a small village nestled in a tucked-away valley of the Ajaches hills. The setting for Picnic 7 is nearby.

reappearing again to meet the Atalaya de Femés track, at just under **1h**. Continue up to the right. Seven minutes up, you reach the summit, where a stupendous view awaits you. The remote (for this island!) little village of Femés lies straight below, huddled around the pass that descends to the Rubicón plain. Fuerteventura and Lobos fill in the backdrop. And from up here you can almost count the colourful volcanoes of Timanfaya. On the other side of the transmitter station, you look down onto Las Breñas, stretching along a raised shelf of cultivation that steps off onto the Rubicón.

Descending to Femés is straightforward. Follow the track all the way down to the first fork-off right, and then remain on this track to the village square (25min down). Hopefully you'll be handsomely repaid with a memorable sunset. Allow one hour to return to Yaiza from the summit. In Yaiza, the bus stop is just at the pedestrian crossing north of the plaza.

Distance: 13km/8mi; 2h30min

Grade: flat and easy, except for the final descent to El Convento, which is vertiginous and dangerous if wet (but this may be omitted)

Equipment: stout shoes with grip (for the descent to El Convento, otherwise comfortable shoes will suffice), sunhat, suncream, cardigan, raingear, picnic, plenty of water, swimwear

How to get there: Playa Blanca- 🚌 to La Hoya (departures from Arrecife and Puerto del Carmen)
To return: 🚌 from La Hoya

I f you're tired of picnicking at the beach and eating sandwiches 'à la grit', then this coastal walk, with its superb unvisited rock pools may be just what you're looking for. Beyond Playa de Janubio you follow a jagged, rocky coastline. There are no more beaches (or people), only natural rock pools — pools to suit all the family — hidden on the lava shelves that jut out into the sea. El Convento is the name given to the impressive sea cave at the end of the walk. It's a beautiful stretch of coastline, only frequented by the local fishermen.

Leave the bus at La Hoya (the junction for Las Breñas) and **start the walk:** follow the road south to the Mirador de las Salinas turn-off, less than **10min** along. It's the first track forking off to the right. Head out to the *mirador*— a point that hangs out over the salt pans and lagoon. From here you have a bird's-eye view over the multitude of tiny white squares of salt and the evaporation ponds that divide up the basin floor, leaving it with a sunset-pink glow. The dark green lagoon enhances this fine setting (see photograph page 61). This particular *salina* (salt pan) produces one-third of Lanzarote's salt. Ornithologists will be happy to know that this is a popular destination for migratory birds as well, and you can expect to find: teal, the cattle egret and little egret (on rare occasions); the grey heron and storks (from time to time); plovers, lapwing, and sparrow hawks (more commonly). Notice also the few derelict windmills down in the basin; these were used for pumping the seawater into the ponds.

The top of the plateau is bare and dusty. From above the lagoon we continue on further south, circling the top of the basin. When you come to the edge of a small but deep ravine (a couple of minutes from the *mirador*), clamber down the steep rocky face at the mouth of it. Take care, it's gravelly. A two-minute descent (possibly on all fours) drops you down onto the basin floor, near the lagoon. Follow the track over on your left to leave the basin. You'll pass by a shed and below a house, to exit through a chained barrier. Come onto the beach track at just over **20min**. Playa de Janubio sweeps around the shoreline below you. From here we head south (left) along the edge of the sea plain, following trails the fishermen use.

Our continuation is a very faint track that lies across the beach track. It begins half a minute up to your left. Soon you'll see the remains of the old Playa Blanca route — a raised stone-built piece of road — below you. Keep close to the sea, so that you don't miss any of those alluring *charcos* (pools) and, where possible, scale down over the rock to check them out. You'll soon discover one that will steal an hour or two of your time. Your own private pool, too!

Along modest cliffs, you follow paths or just plough over the loose lava, and now and then you join up with a stretch of track. If you tire of floundering over all this rocky terrain, head inland for a minute or two and follow the main track along, keeping parallel to the coast. Soon you're looking straight across the stone-strewn Rubicón

The jagged coastline south of the saltpans of Janubio. Beryl-green pools lie ensconced in the low shelves that jut out into the sea. (Car tour 2, Picnic 8; see also photograph page 61.)

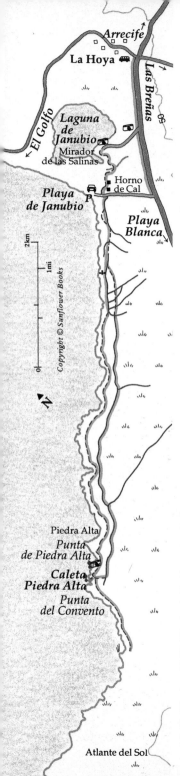

plain to the pointed Ajache hills. In the distance, further along the coast, the abandoned *urbanización* of Atlante del Sol bares itself. Las Breñas is the village you soon see strung out along the edge of an elevated plateau that steps back off this one. The landscape is still and lifeless, and without a drop of colour.

At **35min** into the walk you pass a wooden cross. Stretches of the coastal lava resemble cobblestone paving. About fifteen minutes beyond the cross you begin finding the best pools. So keep an eye out for them. The sea churns up against the shelf, replenishing these pools: obviously, swimming *isn't* recommended in bad weather or when the sea is rough.

At **45min** spot a sea-shelf (from the *edge* of the plain) with a number of pools embedded in it. Two minutes of scrambling over rocks and boulders brings you down to them. This is an excellent spot for children, and the pools are also deep enough for adults. A little over five minutes later, there is another vast shelf with more inviting pools. Finally, a few minutes past this spot, you will find a magnificent solitary pool. All of these emerald-green waterholes are simply irresistible....

Attention is needed at about **1h10min**: Shortly after turning inland (behind a small 'dip') to avoid a mass of lava rock, we pass a cement geographical peg that stands on a point to our right. Here we scramble over all the rock, to the top of the cliffs, for a dramatic coastal overlook. Two inviting green pools lie in what appears to be an inaccessible shelf, immediately below. Behind the pools stands an enormous cave — El Convento — with a

The salt pans of Janubio

'cloistered' entrance opening back into the face of the cliff. A smaller cave sits to its right. Now the problem is: how do we get there?

The safest way down is just beyond the second cave, some three to four minutes round the top of the cliff. You pass over some interesting rock formations, resembling large fragments of broken crockery. Straight off this area of rock, you drop down onto 'lumps' of lava. Meters to the right (and close to the edge of the cliff!), a nose of rock reveals itself. Locating it requires a bit of scouting about. Descend here *with care!* All fours are needed, and this descent is only recommended for *very* surefooted walkers! *Also note: before venturing down, make sure the breakers aren't crashing over the shelf!* When the sea is calm, there is no danger.

This is a superb and sheltered spot to spend the rest of the day. A blow hole lies a further fifteen minutes along the coast, if you can summon up the energy. It's more noticeable for its noise than the spray of water. Find it on a sea-shelf set in the 'U' of the next bay along. The noise gives it away.

The return section of the walk is much easier on the feet: we follow a track that lies just a couple of minutes back off the top of the cliff — slightly inland from the path. Heading back, you get a good view of the Golfo crater — a prominant orange-coloured cone that rises up off the seashore. Remain on the track for the next forty minutes or so, keeping along the coast. Ignore all turn-offs inland. You'll cross several other tracks. Just before reaching the beach track you'll be traipsing across a rocky hillside.

Above the beach, continue up the track to the right and, on the main road, turn left to the junction for La Hoya and your bus stop (1h05min back from El Convento).

9 PLAYA BLANCA • PLAYA DE PAPAGAYO • BARRANCO PARRADO • MACIOT • PLAYA BLANCA

Distance: 28km/17.5mi; 5h

Grade: fairly strenuous because of its length. Total ascent is some 300m/1015ft. There is no shade en route, and it can be *very* hot — so keep this walk for cool overcast days.

Equipment: comfortable shoes or walking boots, cardigan, sunhat, suncream, raingear, picnic, plenty of water, swimwear

How to get there: 🚐 to Playa Blanca (departures from Arrecife and Puerto del Carmen)

To return: 🚐 from Playa Blanca

Short walk: Playa Blanca—Playa de Papagayo—Playa Blanca (2h20min; easy)

S ooner or later you'll discover the island's most beautiful beaches — those east of Playa Blanca, of which Playa de Papagayo is the best known. All are accessible by track, but we meander along the jutting coastline, dipping down into each of these delightful beaches, sampling them as we go. You can bet your boots they'll lure you back another day. With the last of the beaches behind you, you won't see another soul. The landscape is sliced up by ravines and hidden valleys, shut off from the rest of the island by a wall of high hills.

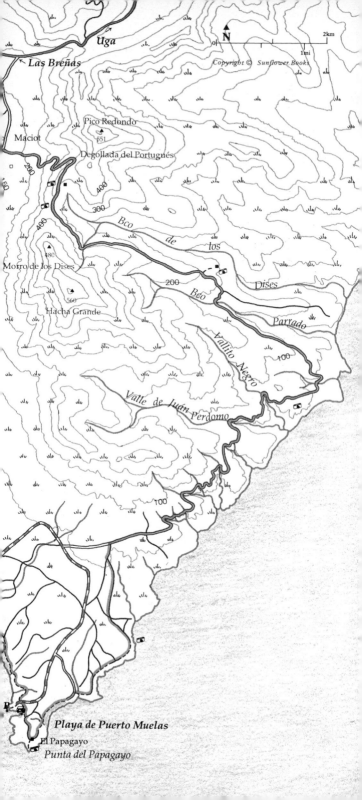

Lanzarote's loveliest beaches, east of Playa Blanca (Picnic 9)

An eyesore of development chewing up the coastline takes up the first half hour of our walk, and there are more such developments on the drawing board. Let's hope that the César Manriques of the island save this unique stretch of coastline. A new road is in the pipeline for Playa de Papagayo, so the map may not be 100% accurate — however, the route is very straightforward. **Start off** by

Camels, once beasts of burden and an important part of the rural scene, lead a much more leisurely life these days ... carrying tourists to the famous Montaña del Fuego. This camel train is homeward-bound

following the road heading east through the resort. When the asphalt road ends at a T-junction, bear right to follow a gravel road along the coast. Some **20min** en route a detour takes us up to a well-restored circular castle tower (Castillo de las Coloradas), bearing the date 1769. To reach it, leave the track/road just after passing a little house near the sea; follow a faint track up to the tower. Off this headland you have a good view back to Playa Blanca and towards the superb beaches scooped out of the open bay on your left which culminates in Punta de Papagayo. Then a tarred road returns us to the track.

Turn right along it and head up through a large *urbanización* (under construction). Then head down to the beach, the Playa de Afe, just over the hill. Walk along the beach to your left. This stony beach is the ugly duckling of the *playas*. At the end of it a path takes you up (with a slight scramble) to the sea-plain above, where you find a clear path over to Playa Mujeres. Low spiny *Launaea* lies scattered across the plain. Wherever you find *Launaea* there's usually *cosco* nearby. *Cosco* turns a vivid wine colour under drought conditions (see *Landscapes of Fuerteventura*, page 40), and great colonies of it stain the inclines. The fruit of this plant was used to make a substitute *gofio* (normally a roasted corn flour), and was used as a thickening agent in soups, etc.

Some **45min** into the walk the unspoilt Playa Mujeres is in sight. This lovely open beach stretches across the mouth of a shallow *barranco*. El Papagayo, the only sign of civilisation out here, is the handful of derelict buildings near the point. Your path drops down into a small gravelly *barranco* and mounts a faint track which leads you down onto the golden sandy beach. You look back into the windswept hills of Los Ajaches. Near the end of the beach scale the sandy bank to remount the crest — a steep, slippery two-minute climb on sand, followed by loose gravel. Continuing along the top of the crest, you dip in and out of small *barrancos* which empty out into concealed coves below.

Playa de los Pozos is the next of the larger beaches. Straight after crossing a track, you clamber down a narrow streambed to reach it. Ascend the goats' path that edges around the hillside at the end of the beach, and once again you're above the sea. If the way appears vertiginous, scramble up onto the plain straight up from the beach. More enticing coves reveal themselves. Most days you'll find they're occupied; this coastline is well and truly 'discovered' — but, fortunately, far from crowded. Soon the old settlement of Papagayo reappears on the crest of the ridge ahead; its crumbled stone buildings leave one assuming that it's uninhabited. Circling behind a couple of coves you reach the top of the crest (**1h10min**) — and find that, to the contrary, El Papagayo *is* inhabited ... by hippies. A rust-brown and deep mauve-coloured rocky promontory separates the two dazzling coves on either side of you. From here you have a striking view of the smooth-faced inland hills, as well as along the string of beaches you've just visited (see photograph page 64). If you're only doing the Short walk, you'll have plenty of time to sample these paradisial beaches and coves; otherwise, you'll only have time for a couple of them.

Continuing on, follow the path curving around the walls of Playa de Papagayo. You look down onto the beach and a number of tents fastened to the face of the hill. Ice-plants and *cosco* patch the slope. (If this path looks unnerving, make your way around via the top of the crest.) Shortly meet a track from your left and follow it out to Punta del Papagayo. It passes a pillbox a couple of minutes along and then swings sharply back left. The point is just beyond the shelter. *Don't* go too near to the edge of the cliffs on windy days! Fuerteventura is now closer than ever, and the dark 'pimply' island of Lobos is made more prominent by the sand dunes of Corralejo in the background. Back to your left you can see Puerto del Carmen and Arrecife — a vast expanse of white trimming the sloping sea-plain. A staggered chain of cone-shaped hills runs down the centre of the island.

A few minutes below the pillbox (at about **1h20min**) the track fizzles out onto yet another beach — Playa de Puerto Muelas. This secluded beach is the most popular out here. Could the fact that it's the (unofficial) nudist beach have something to do with it? Five minutes along the beach (trying not to look left or right), reach the carpark. Follow the track north to the next cove, a minute over, and then ascend to the top of the cliffs beyond it. Pieces of track lead you along these cliffs. Ten minutes from the last beach you come onto a clearer track and overlook a rocky cove set at the mouth of a deep ravine. Here we turn up left, keeping straight up (bear left at the fork you encounter and pass through an intersection), until we meet a T-junction (at about **1h50min**).

Bearing right at the junction we now sidle along the hills, disappearing further out 'into the sticks'. No more beaches, no more people ... but perhaps a goatherd and a handful of goats. Ignoring all tracks that fork off left and right, we remain on a generally even contour. Gradually ascending, we look straight off the sloping shelf onto the sea. The way curves back into a number of *barrancos* that slice inland, and soon it's no longer passable by vehicles (from this side). Some **2h20min** en route, drop down into a good-sized gulley and cross a wide gravelly streambed. The countryside can be surprisingly green out here in winter and spring. Still no sign of life, nor any trees ... a desolate spot indeed.

Tías comes into full view, its elevated slopes speckled with white buildings. The surrounding hills have subsided into a gentle rolling landscape. A brief descent takes you down to another *barranco* crossing. Now the hard work begins — a 60-minute uphill slog follows. We wind our way up into the largest of the valleys so far encountered. Dandelions and *Echium* add their golds and purples to the spring greenery. Some five minutes uphill from the streambed crossing, come to an intersection and bear left. A few minutes later, you'll see a shepherds' crumbled outpost on a rocky outcrop above the track. On a windy day it serves as a good picnic shelter. There's also a large colony of ice plants here. This plant was once traded for its soda content. Pico Redondo (551m/1800ft) is the peak rising up out of the next valley over on your right. Nearer the pass, you encounter the first trees — some rather scrawny examples of *Solanaceae* (the tobacco family) — scattered along the side of the road.

A fantastic viewpoint (where you're often hit by a gale-force wind), awaits you when you cross the pass ... or are blown over it ... and descend to the Playa Blanca wasteland. You look back down the valley and over the stone-covered Rubicón plain that fans out across the southwestern corner of the island. Below sits the tiny hamlet of Maciot — a manicured patch of gardens completely lost in this dark, dismal corner. Playa Blanca is to your left and El Faro (the lighthouse) de la Punta Pechiguera to the right of it. A goats' pen made of 44 gallon drums sits at the top of the pass (**3h35min** en route). Dropping quickly now, you twist down the sheer escarpment. Twenty minutes down, exit onto the gravel Las Breñas/Femés—Playa Blanca road and turn left along it. Keep straight on after the cement works and join the main road just above Playa Blanca. Two minutes down to the left, reach a roundabout and the bus stop.

Index

Geographical names comprise the only entries in this index; for other entries, see Contents on page 3. **Bold-face** type indicates a photograph; *italic* type indicates a map reference.

Arrecife
Town plan: touring map
Arrieta 18, **46**
Atalaya de Femés 15, 55, *56*, **57**
Casas la Breña 39, *41*
Castillo de Santa Bárbara 23, *44*, 46
Castillo de las Coloradas *62*, 65
Cueva de los Verdes 16, 19
El Convento (cave) 58, *60*, 61
El Golfo 22, **23**, **24**, 25, 28
El Jable (plain) 23, 36
El Papagayo 29, *63*, 65, 66
Ermita de las Nieves 43, *44*
Femés 15, 25, 29, 55, *56*, 57
Guatiza 16
Guinate 38, 39, *40*
Haría 16, 22
Islote de Hilario 27
Jameos del Agua 16, 18, **20**
Janubio *see* Salinas de Janubio
La Caleta de Famara 24, *44*
La Degollada **57**
La Geria (valley) 25, 30, **51**, *52*
La Graciosa 14, 31-3, *33*
La Hoya 28, 58, *60*, 61
La Montañeta 50, *52-3*
La Quemada (crater) 39, *41*, 42
La Santa 26
Las Breñas 29
Los Ajaches (hills) 28, **57**, 65
Los Hervideros (*mirador*) 28
Los Valles 23
Mácher 50, *52-3*
Máguez 14, 21, 38, 39, *40*
Mala 18, 43, *45*
Malpais de la Corona ('Bad-lands') 19, 20, 41
Mancha Blanca 26, 47, *49*, **49**
Masdache 30
Mirador del Río 16, **17**, 21, *40*
Montaña Bermeja *33*
Montaña Blanca *46*, **47**, *48*, 49
Montaña Clara 21, 32
Montaña Corona **22**, 39, *40*, 41, **42**
Montaña Guardilama 15, 50,

51, *53*, **53**, 54
Montañas del Fuego **18-19**, 25, 27, **64**
Monumento al Campesino **21**, 25
Mozaga 16, 24, 26
Orzola 16, 20, 31
Pico de las Nieves 14
Playa Blanca 25, 29, *62*, 67
Playa de Afe *62*, 65
Playa de Famara 21, *44*
Playa de Janubio 59, *60*
Playa de Papagayo 15, *62*, **64**, 66
Playa de Puerto Muelas *62*, 66
Playa del Ambar 32, *33*
Playa del Risco 21, 36, *40*
Playa de la Madera 47, *48*
Playa de las Conchas **34**, *33*
Playa de las Malvas 47, *48*
Playa de los Pozos *62*, 65
Playa Mujeres *62*, 65
Puerto del Carmen 53
Town plan: touring map
Punta del Papagayo 15, *63*, 66
Punta Mujeres 18
Risco de Famara 14, **17**, 21, 35, *40*
Salinas de Janubio 15, 28, 29, 58, **59**, *60*, **61**
Salinas del Río 21, 36, **37**, **38**, *40*
San Bartolomé 24, 25
Tahiche 16
Tao 26
Teguise 16, 24, 43, *44*, 46
Tiagua 26
Tías 24
Timanfaya National Park **18-19**, 25, **51**
Tinajo 25, 26, 47, *49*
Torrecilla de Domingo *40*, **42**
Uga 14, 30, 50, *52*
Urbanización Famara 24, *44*
Valle del Palomo 43, *45*, **46**
Yaiza 25, 27, 55, *56*, 57
Ye 35, 39, *40*, 42

Landscapes of
FUERTEVENTURA
a countryside guide

Noel Rochford

SUNFLOWER
BOOKS

Dedicated to Roy and Stephen

First published 1989 by
Sunflower Books
12 Kendrick Mews
London SW7 3HG, UK

*Above: a molino;
a molina is shown
on the title page*

ISBN 0-948513-48-9

Important note to the reader _____

I have tried to ensure that the descriptions and maps in this book are error-free at press date. The book will be updated, where necessary, whenever future printings permit. It will be very helpful for me to receive your comments (sent in care of the publishers, please) for the updating o future printings. I also rely on those who use this book — especially walkers — to take along a good supply of common sense when they explore. Conditions change fairly rapidly on Fuerteventura, and ***storm damage or bulldozing may make a route unsafe at any time.*** If the route is not as I outline it here, and your way ahead is not secure, return to the point of departure. ***Never attempt to complete a tour or walk under hazardous conditions!*** Please read carefully the notes on pages 7 to 13, as well as the introductory comments at the beginning of each tour and walk (regarding road conditions, equipment, grade, distances and time, etc). Explore ***safely***, while at the same time respecting the beauty of the countryside.

Photographs by the author
Maps by John Theasby and Pat Underwood
Drawings by Sharon Rochford
Printed and bound in the UK by A Wheaton and Co Ltd, Exeter

D5/KH

❀ Contents

Preface   5
  Acknowledgements   6
  Useful books   6

Introduction   7
  Getting about on the island   7
  Picnicking   7
  Touring   8
  Walking   9
    Dogs and other nuisances   10
    Weather   10
    Where to stay   11
    What to take   11
  Spanish for walkers and motorists   12
  A country code for walkers and motorists   13

Picnic suggestions   14

Car tours   15
  The best of Fuerteventura (Tour 1)   15
  Punta de Jandía and the west coast (Tour 2)   22
  Northern landscapes (Tour 3)   25

Walks   30
  1 Around Lobos   30
  2 El Cotillo • Casas de Majanicho • Corralejo   33
  3 Montaña Tindaya   38
  4 Llanos de la Concepción • Embalse de los Molinos •
     Morro de la Cueva • Llanos de la Concepción   41
  5 Barranco de las Peñitas (Vega de Río de Palmas)   45
  6 Puerto de la Peña • Barranco de la Madre del Agua •
     Peña Horadada • Puerto de la Peña   48
  7 Pico de la Zarza   53
  8 Barranco Gran Valle • Degollada de Cofete • Playa de
     Cofete • Barranco Gran Valle   57

Index   60

Touring map   after Index
Transport timetables   on touring map
Town plans   on touring map

3

Betancuria

 # Preface

Fuerteventura is different from all the other islands in the Canaries. Being the closest to Africa, there's a definite taste of the Sahara about it. The landscape is thirsty, barren and severe. Here peace and quiet prevails. The countryside is lonely but warm, bleak but friendly and, in its own way, beautiful.

In two things this island excels and outdoes all the others in the archipelago: it has the best beaches and the best climate. Beaches are what Fuerteventura is all about; they 'sell' the island to tourists. You'll find mile upon mile of untouched golden sand, great billowing white sand dunes, foaming surf, and quiet turquoise coves. If you're after sea and sun, this is the island for you! Windsurfers, too, are just discovering the perfect winds to enjoy their hobby.

Even though the landscape changes little, it's pleasant to tour Fuerteventura by car, since there's little traffic on the roads. The pace is relaxing and the landscape timeless. The island's beauty spots are tucked away, often out of sight. I hope this new addition to the 'Landscapes' Series will help you find them.

And just in case you get tired of the beaches (which is fairly unlikely), or there's an overcast, cool day, there is some walking to be enjoyed on Fuerteventura. You needn't be an inveterate hiker: there are walks to suit all appetites — rambles across the old worn hills, fairly easy mountain ascents, a seaside hike and, for explorers, rocky *barrancos* in which to flounder. Even the picnic spots will help you get better acquainted with the island. There are hidden streams, palm groves, and crystal-clear lagoons just waiting to be discovered. Lobos — the tiny island of 'anthills' — is another world again. It's a charmer.

Fuerteventura is the richest of the islands in Guanche relics (sorry, Gran Canaria). Few people are aware of this.

5

The island is littered with Guanche settlements — all untouched. Unfortunately, they are also unprotected and crumbling away. Admittedly, most are hard to distinguish or are well off the beaten track; hence I've only covered a couple of these sites in the book.

Tourism, after having side-stepped this island for so many years, has suddenly struck like a bolt of lightning, and the populace is still reeling from the blow. Being reserved in character by nature, they are still very wary of it all — as we all know, tourism brings with it a lot more than money.... So you may not find the Fuerteventurans as open or as friendly as other Canarians. Speaking some Spanish can make a big difference, especially amongst the village folk and those not involved in tourism.

Landscapes of Fuerteventura will, I hope, give you a better insight into this newly-booming tourist mecca.

Acknowledgements

I would like to express my thanks to the following people for their much-appreciated help:

Andrés Valerón Hernandez, and Claudia, from the Patronato de Turismo de Fuerteventura;

Enrique Abascal, for his 'taxi service' and continual offers of help;

Marie Carmen, from the Cabildo library, for searching the entire shelves for me.

Very special thanks to Sr Francisco Navaro Artiles, who gave up hours of his precious time to help with all my queries, as well as chauffeur me around the island; to Sra 'Maruca' Rodriguez for her kindness; and to my sister Sharon for her excellent drawings.

Finally, thanks to my family, friends, and publishers, who always support my work and travels.

Useful books

Bramwell, D and Bramwell, Z *Wild Flowers of the Canary Islands.* London, Stanley Thornes Ltd.

Bramwell, D and Bramwell, Z *Historia Natural de las Islas Canarias.* Editorial Rueda.

Vicente Araña and Juán Carracedo, *Los volcanoes de las Islas Canarias, II: Lanzarote y Fuerteventura* (with English text). Editorial Rueda.

Carlos Javier Taranilla, *Fuerteventura.* Editorial Everest.

Casa Coronel, in La Oliva

❀ Introduction

Getting about on the island

On Fuerteventura one has no choice but to hire a vehicle, if you want to travel about the island independently. The local bus service is far too limited.

Car hire here is expensive, compared with other islands in the Canaries; however, sharing will cut the cost. **Taxis** are also expensive, because you have to travel fairly long distances (for instance, just to reach your resort from the airport). Here again, sharing lessens the blow. Agree on a price before setting out by taxi, and don't be afraid to bargain politely.

Coach tours are easy to arrange and get you to all the tourist points of interest, but never off the beaten track. The **local bus service** is seldom used by tourists, so you'll be something of a curiosity here! The bus drivers are friendly and obliging. If you do get the opportunity, it's worth doing one of the long, slow hauls once! You'll find **transport timetables** on the touring map.

Picnicking

Most tourists come here for the beaches and the peace and quiet. There are enough beautiful beaches on this island to visit a different one each day for a month. Many of them are off the beaten track, and this means taking along a picnic hamper ... if you intend to spend the day there.

Finding other picnic spots, however, is a different story. There are no 'organised' picnic places on Fuerteventura, unlike some of the other Canary Islands. The picnic settings I've suggested are therefore natural beauty spots I've discovered on my walks. My own personal favourite is Lobos.

On page 14 you will find my suggestions for six lovely picnics, together with all the information you need to reach them. *Note that picnic numbers correspond to walk*

7

numbers; thus you can quickly find the general location on the island by referring to the pull-out touring map (where the walks are outlined in white). Most of the spots I've chosen are very easy to reach, and I suggest where you can park (🚍), walking times, and views or setting. Beside the picnic title, you'll also find a map reference: the exact location of the picnic spot is shown on this large-scale *walking* map by the symbol *P*. Some of the picnics are also illustrated; if so, the photograph reference follows the map reference.

Please glance over the comments before you start off on your picnic: if some walking is involved, remember to wear sensible shoes and to **take a sunhat (☼** = picnic in full sun). It's a good idea to take along a plastic groundsheet as well, in case the ground is damp.

If you are travelling to your picnic by bus, be sure to verify departure times in advance. Although there are timetables in this book, they *do* change from time to time, without prior warning. **If you are travelling to your picnic by** car, be extra vigilant off the main roads.

All picnickers should read the country code on page 13 and go quietly in the countryside. *Buen provecho!*

Touring

Most visitors to Fuerteventura hire a vehicle for all or part of their stay. As it is quite expensive here, it's a good idea to share with friends. Do shop around, while at the same time bearing in mind that cheapest is not always best! Always check your vehicle in advance and point out any existing dents, scratches, etc. Ask for all the conditions and insurance cover in writing, in English. Check to make sure you have a sound spare tyre and all the necessary tools. Be sure to get the office *and the after-hours* telephone numbers of the car hire firm and carry them with you. If you're not 100% happy about the car, don't take it. Finally, make a note of exactly what you're signing for, if you pay by credit card. *Important:* Leave nothing of value in your car, and always lock it. Car theft is on the increase. Park near to other cars, or where you can keep an eye on your vehicle.

The touring notes are brief: they contain little history or information readily available in tourist office leaflets (which you can obtain free of charge). The main tourist centres and towns are not described either, for the same reason. Instead, I concentrate on the 'logistics' of touring: times and distances, road conditions, and seeing places many tourists miss. Most of all I emphasise possibilities for **walking** and **picnicking**. While some of the references to picnics off the beaten track (indicated by the symbol **P** in the touring notes) may not be suitable during a long car tour, you may see a landscape that you would like to explore at leisure another day, when you've more time to stretch your legs.

The large fold-out touring map is designed to be held out opposite the touring notes and contains all the information you will need outside the towns. The two largest resorts on the island are Corralejo and Jandía, so I have based the drives around these two centres. The best car tour, in my opinion, is Tour 1 — with the Jandía Peninsula tacked on to it. **Town plans** with exits for motorists are on the touring map. Remember to allow plenty of time for **visits**, and to take along **warm clothing** as well as some food and drink, in case you are delayed. The **distances** quoted in the notes are *cumulative* from the departure point. A **key to the symbols** used in the touring notes on pages 15 to 29 is on the touring map.

All motorists should read the country code on page 13 and go quietly in the countryside. *Buen viaje!*

Walking

Fuerteventura is a large island; however it does not boast a great variety of landscapes. For this reason the walks in this book are *not* distributed all over the island. Instead, I have covered only the more scenic countryside. As you will see, Fuerteventura *does* offer the walker some picturesque corners.

There are walks in this book for everyone. To choose a walk that appeals to you, you might begin by looking at the touring map inside the back cover. Here you can see at a glance the overall terrain, the roads, and the location of the walks. Flipping through the book, you will see that there is at least one photograph for every walk. Having selected one or two potential excursions from the map and the photographs, turn to the relevant walk. At the top of the page you will find planning information: distance/time, grade, equipment, and how to get there. If the grade and equipment specifications are beyond your scope, don't despair! *There's sometimes a short or alternative version of a walk*, and in most cases these are far less demanding. *If you want a really easy walk, you need look no further than the picnic suggestions on page 14.*

When you are on your walk, you will find that the text

begins with an introduction to the overall landscape and then quickly turns to a detailed description of the route. The **large-scale maps** (generally 1:40,000 or 1:50,000) have been specially annotated to show key landmarks. Times are given for reaching certain points in the walk. **Note: I am a very fit, very fast walker!** So if you are a beginner, or if you prefer a more leisurely pace, a walk may **take you more than twice as long!** The most important factor is *consistency* of times, and I suggest that you compare your pace with mine on one or two short walks, before you set off on a long hike. Don't forget to take transport connections into account!

Note that roads and tracks on the walking **maps** correspond to those on the touring map. **Scale** of miles and **north/south** orientation is included on each map. Below is a key to the **symbols** used to indicate landmarks:

🎥	best views	**P**	picnic spot (see page 7)
♦/⊥	church, chapel/shrine	❢	danger; danger of vertigo!
◄●	spring, tank, etc	🚗	car parking
▢▢▢	habitations	■	building in the text
⚡	pylon, wires	▬	walls (usually stone)

The walks in the north can be done using local tranport. Those in the centre of the island require private transport and, accordingly, I have made them circular walks. In the south, the hikes are virtually on your doorstep. No guides are required for any of the walks; you cross open countryside. Climbing Pico de la Zarza, however, needs a cloudless day; otherwise you're asking for trouble. One walk which I have purposely left *out* of the book is the unique stretch of beach from Morro del Jable to Costa Calma (23km; 3h45min *my time, remember*). This needs no explanations, and nearly everyone does some part of it. If you're fit try the whole stretch. What a ramble!

Dogs and other nuisances

The only way **dogs** will bother you is by following you and tripping you up! Goatherds' dogs are all bark and no bite. Usually, where there are goats and sheep, you find **ticks** as well. Fuerteventura is no exception, but because there isn't much long grass they are less of a nuisance here than elsewhere.

Weather

Fuerteventura has a climate to match its beaches: The mean average temperature is 19°C, with fairly hot summer days and a very mild winter ... to say nothing of a healthy 2900+ hours of sunshine per year!

November to March are the best walking months. Sun-seekers, I'm sorry to say that you *will* get cloudy days, some quite miserable and fresh — just right for a long hike. *Wet* days — from the blessed (for the islanders) west- to southwest winds — are quite a phenomenon here; they arrive about as frequently as a *real* summer in England (when everybody remembers the year...).

The main winds are the northeast to north, which can be very strong in spring and summer — just right for wind-surfing, and the bothersome southeast to south — a dry hot wind off the Sahara that fills the air with dust. These winds only last for two to three days, but can be very unpleasant. In summer, mists (from the trade winds) are common over the Jandía mountains, but they won't affect your beach days. So really, all you've got to worry about is the sun and the heat. Don't overdo it on your first day!

Where to stay

There are two main resorts on the island: Corralejo in the north and Jandía in the south. For walkers neither has the advantage over the other. There are also a number of sea-side villages where you can find apartments if you're travelling independently: try El Cotillo, El Castillo, Las Playitas, Tarajalejo, La Lajita, and Ginijinamar. But, as with Puerto del Rosario, finding unreserved accommodation in 'the season' is difficult.

The bus service is better *going to* Puerto del Rosario than travelling *from* it. There is no accommodation specifically for tourists in the capital, but don't let that worry you; it is the least attractive and least friendly place on the island. Morro del Jable, Corralejo and Costa Calma are all architectural nightmares ... but they do straddle superb beaches.

What to take

If you're already on Fuerteventura when you find this book, and you don't have any special equipment such as walking boots or a rucksack, you can still do some of the walks — or buy yourself some equipment in one of the sports shops. Don't attempt the more difficult walks without the proper gear. For each walk in the book, the *mini-mum* equipment is listed.

Please bear in mind that I've not done *every* walk in this book under *all* weather conditions. Use your good judgement to modify my equipment list according to the season!

You may find the following checklist useful:

walking boots (which *must* be broken-in and comfortable)	up-to-date transport timetables
waterproof rain gear (outside summer months)	lightweight water containers
	small rucksack
long-sleeved shirt (sun protection)	long trousers, tight at the ankles
bandages and band-aids	protective sun cream
plastic plates, cups, etc	knives and openers
anorak (zip opening)	2 lightweight cardigans
extra pair of socks	spare bootlaces
plastic groundsheet	torch
sunhat	whistle
insect repellant	compass

Spanish for walkers and motorists

In the tourist centres you hardly need know any Spanish at all. But once you are out in the countryside, a few words of the language will be helpful, especially if you lose your way. It may also help you 'break through' the natural reserve of the Fuerteventurans.

Here's an — almost — foolproof way to communicate in Spanish. First, memorise the few short key questions and their possible answers, given below. Then, when you have your 'mini-speech' memorised, always ask the many questions you can concoct from it **in such a way that you get a "sí" (yes) or "no" answer.** *Never* ask an open-ended question such as "Where is the main road?". Instead, ask the question and then *suggest the most likely answer yourself.* For instance: "Good day, sir. Please — where is the path to Cofete? *Is it straight ahead?*" Now, unless you get a "sí" response, try: "*Is it to the left?*" If you go through the list of answers to your own question, you should eventually get a "sí" response!

Following are the most likely situations in which you may have to practice your Spanish. The dots (...) show where you will fill in the name of your destination. Ask a local person — perhaps someone at your hotel — to help you with the pronunciation of place names.

Asking the way
Key questions

English	Spanish	Pronunciation
Good day, sir (madam, miss).	Buenos días, señor (señora, señorita).	**Boo**-eh-nohs **dee**-ahs, sen-**yor** (sen-**yor**-ah, sen-yor-**ee**-tah).
Please — where is	Por favor — dónde está	**Poor** fah-**vor** — **dohn**-day es-**tah**
the road to ...?	la carretera a ...?	lah cah-reh-**teh**-rah ah ...?
the footpath to...?	la senda de ...?	lah **sen**-dah day ...?
the way to ...?	el camino a ...?	el cah-**mee**-noh ah ...?
the bus stop?	la parada?	lah pah-**rah**-dah?
Many thanks.	Muchas gracias.	**Moo**-chas **gra**-thee-ahs.

Possible answers

English	Spanish	Pronunciation
here?	aquí?	ah-**kee**?
there?	allá?	ayl-**yah**?
straight ahead?	todo recto?	**toh**-doh **rayk**-toh?
behind?	detrás?	day-**tras**?
right?	a la derecha?	ah lah day-**ray**-chah?
left?	a la izquierda?	ah lah eeth-kee-**er**-dah?
above?	arriba?	ah-**ree**-bah?
below?	abajo?	ah-**bah**-hoh?

Asking a taxidriver to take you somewhere and return for you, or asking a taxi driver to meet you at a certain place and time

English	Spanish	Pronunciation
Please —	Por favor —	**Poor** fah-**vor** —
take us to …	llévanos a …	l-**yay**-vah-nohs ah…
and return for us	y venga buscarnos	ee **vain**-gah boos-**kar**-nohs
at (place) at (time).	a … a … .*	ah (place) ah (time).*

*Just point out the time on your watch.

A country code for walkers and motorists

- **Do not light fires.**
- **Do not frighten animals.** The goats and sheep you may encounter on your walks are not tame. By making loud noises, or by trying to touch or photograph the animals, you may cause them to run in fear and be hurt.
- **Walk quietly** through all hamlets and villages.
- **Leave all gates just as you find them.** Although you may not see any animals, the gates *do* have a purpose — generally to keep goats or sheep in (or out of) an area.
- **Protect all wild and cultivated plants.** Don't try to pick wild flowers or uproot saplings. Obviously fruit and other crops are someone's private property and should not be touched. ***Never walk over cultivated land.***
- **Take all your litter away with you.**
- **Walkers — *Do not take risks!*** This is the most important point of all. Do not attempt walks beyond your capacity, and do not wander off the paths described here if there is any sign of mist or if it is late in the day. **Do not walk alone** (four is the best walking group), and *always* tell a responsible person *exactly* where you are going and what time you plan to return. Remember, if you become lost or injure yourself, it may be a long time before you are found. On any but a very short walk close to villages, be sure to take a compass, whistle, torch, extra water and warm clothing — as well as some high-energy food, like chocolate. Read and re-read the important note on page 2, as well as guidelines on grade and equipment for each walk you plan to do!

Picnic suggestions

1   LOBOS (map page 31; photograph page 32)

by 🚢: 10-15min on foot. Ferry from El Cotillo to Lobos.
Head left straight off the jetty; less than 10min along, spot a path branching off left, into sand dunes. This leads to lovely Playa de la Calera. If you prefer swimming off rocks, try the stunning setting of Casas El Puertito, 5min from the jetty (to the right). Both are superb, tranquil spots. ✪

2   EL COTILLO (map pages 34-5, photograph page 37)

by 🚗: 5-10min on foot. Park off the side of the lighthouse road, north of El Cotillo.
Picnic at any of the delightful turquoise coves or on the dunes near the lighthouse. ✪

5   BARRANCO DE LAS PEÑITAS (map page 45, photographs pages 25 and 47)

by 🚗: 10-20min on foot. Park beyond the last houses on the Presa de las Peñitas road (south of Vega de Río de Palmas), off curve above reservoir.
Skirt the reservoir to the right to reach the dam wall, and use notes on page 46 to descend (with care) to the chapel, which offers the only shade in this sun-baked setting. ✪

6a   BARRANCO DE LA MADRE DEL AGUA (map page 49, photograph page 51)

by 🚗: 10-15min on foot. Park in Ajuy (9km west of Pajara on the Puerto de la Peña road), just before a roadside house above the barranco.
Enter the bed of the barranco down to your right and walk left along it to the tiny ravine that cuts back off this one, a few minutes along. It's choked with palms and has a lovely little brook with a footbridge. Picnicking in a setting like this is rare indeed on Fuerteventura!

Tree
candelabra

6b   CALETA NEGRA (map page 49)

by 🚗: 15-20min on foot. Park in Puerto de la Peña.
*Follow the old port path out of the village (right). When it ends, climb to the top of the crest above, and continue along the coast. In 3min overlook Caleta Negra. The notes on page 52 tell you how to reach the old port and sea-caves. This descent is only for the **very** sure-footed picnicker!* ✪

8   COFETE (map page 56)

by 🚗 (jeep or 4-wheel drive only): 0-5min on foot. Take the first turn-off left outside Cofete hamlet to the beaches of Cofete and Barlovento de Jandía. Park on the beach.
Picnic anywhere. Note that the sea is very dangerous; treat it with respect. No shade. ✪

1 THE BEST OF FUERTEVENTURA

Morro del Jable • La Pared • Betancuria • La Antigua • Gran Tarajal • Las Playitas • Morro del Jable

190km/118mi; 5 hours driving; Exit A from Morro del Jable

En route: P5, 6a, 6b; Walks 4, 5, 6, 7

The main north—south road is generally good. However, between La Antigua and Tarajalejo it's rough and full of potholes. Inland roads are good, but narrow. Between Pájara and Vega de Río de Palmas the road is quite high and winding; some people will find this stretch unnerving, since there is not always a roadside barrier. Watch out for animals on the roads in the countryside, and for pedestrians in the villages. Local people seem to drive very fast, so stay alert. Note also that it can be very windy. The only petrol stations en route (closed Sundays and holidays) are in Tuineje and Gran Tarajal.

Opening hours: Museo Sacreo (Betancuria): 10.00-14.30 and 15.30-17.30 daily except Sundays. You can also obtain the key to the cathedral here at the museum.

This drive takes you to some of the best sights on the island, from the most stunning beaches to the most picturesque valleys. You will be treated not only to the beauty spots, but also to the geographical and geological wonders of the island. And the final ingredient to flavour this tour to perfection is the little village of Betancuria — Fuerteventura's ancient capital.

Leaving Morro del Jable we take the GC640 as far north as the junction for La Pared. Out of the eyesore of development, we wind in and out of the deep bare *barrancos* that cleave the mountainous backbone of the Jandía Peninsula. Pico de la Zarza (806m/2645ft), the island's highest summit, can be seen at the end of both the Vinamar and Butihonda valleys. It's a modest peak that rises a mere shoulder above its off-siders. On a fine day, however, you can have a most enjoyable hike here — see Walk 7.

Close on 16km out of Morro del Jable, just as we leave **Barranco Los Canarios** (✕), we round a corner and come to a stunning view over the captivating Playa de Sotavento de Jandía★ — the queen of Fuerteventura's beaches (see pages 17 and 21). A track forks right off the corner here and descends to the beach below. Pull over onto this track, so that you can really appreciate this magnificent coastal vista or, if you want to get closer still, take the track opposite the Restaurante Bei Michael a kilometre further on and follow it towards the sea; you'll end up atop the dunes. The beach widens into an expansive sand bar, and the sea will no doubt be dotted with a myriad of colourful windsurfs. In the background the coastline curves sharply right, and off the beach rise the giant sand hills of the Pared isthmus — through which we are about to pass.

15

Just before we turn off the main road, at the end of the dunes, we pass through **Costa Calma** (25km ⛰️⛰️🏠✕), another *urbanización* constructed without regard to preserving the beauty of the coast. Some 27km from Morro del Jable, we turn off left for La Pared, at a junction 1.5km beyond Costa Calma (not signposted). After 5km we reach **La Pared** (⛰️⛰️🏠✕), which sits in a desolate and naked landscape on the outskirts of the dunes. This scattering of buildings looks sad, neglected and unsightly, so let's head on to Pájara. The cloud-catching hills rising on our right, of which Montaña Cardón (691m/2265ft) is the highest, cut off the west coast from the rest of the island. A few kilometres out, we encounter the first of the 'zona militar' signs — all of which are barely discernible. This prohibited area (a firing range) stretches along almost all the way to Pájara, so don't drive onto any tracks or roads branching off towards the coast.

We pass the quiet cultivated valley of Huertas de Chilegua, and the road climbs into smooth rounded hills sparse of vegetation. (The absence of side-railings on this road may make it unnerving for some people.) These ochre-coloured mounds are of the basement complex, ie the oldest hill formations. Descending to another isolated farmstead, you'll see small earthen reservoirs in the valley floor. These are called *presas secas* ('dry reservoirs'), because they have been constructed to catch the water that comes down the *barrancos*, but they do not retain it. The water passes through the permeable soil into wells which have been sunk some 17-20m (about 60ft) below the ground in front of these *presas*. The small metal windmills you see everywhere are used to pump this water up to ground level again (see page 29).

Closer to Pájara the hills open out into a vast depression. Meet a junction (54km) and turn left, to descend to Ajuy/Puerto de la Peña. Rounding a corner, we look down into a valley lush with palm trees, tamarisk shrubs and garden plots. Notice the small ravine crammed with palm trees cutting back off it, into the hills running down on the right. This ravine (**P**6) boasts the only permanently flowing stream on Fuerteventura. It's only a trickle, but the picnic spot is enchanting (see page 51).

Puerto de la Peña (63km), a small village set on the edge of a black sand beach, is one of two fishing settlements on the west coast. Few tourists venture over to the dramatically-sited ancient port here. It hides in a bay some ten minutes' walk around the coast to the south of the village. I'd suggest you use the notes for **Picnic 6b** to discover the huge sea caverns that open out back off this port ...*but only if you are **extremely** sure-footed.*

From Puerto de la Peña return to the junction and keep straight on to **Pájara** (74km ✝ ✕ and swimming pool). This is a large farming community surrounded by hills. The shady village is a welcoming sight, with its abundance of trees and small colourful gardens. Don't miss the church

Playa de Sotavento de Jandía — Fuerteventura's finest beach

here; it is especially noteworthy for the striking 'Aztec' stone-carved decoration above the main entrance. Quite a curiosity because, apart from a similar lot of sculptures in La Oliva, these carvings are unique in the Canary Islands. The two naves inside the church date back to 1645 and 1687, while the carving over the door is thought to date from the 1500s.

Leaving Pájara take the road for Vega de Río de Palmas; it's at the left of the church. Again we ascend into the hills, climbing on a narrow winding road that hugs the sheer inclines (again, some people might find this road un-nerving). There are excellent views back over the Barranco de Pájara. The Degollada de los Granadillos (with parking for *one* car only) is the pass that takes us over a solid spur of rock that juts out into the valley below. It's a dangerous corner for parking! From this pass you have a superb outlook over to the enclosing rocky ridges.

Soon, descending, we look down onto the Presa de las Peñitas, a muddy reservoir lodged in the 'V' of the Barranco de las Peñitas. The reservoir looks deeper than it is; it's only about 1 metre (3ft) deep, since it has filled up with silt. Groves of tamarisk huddle around the tail of the *presa*, and that's a good spot from which to do some bird-watching. Green gardens step the sides of the slopes, and palm trees complement the scene. Below the reservoir lies a sheer-sided rocky ravine, the ideal hiding place for the chapel dedicated to the island's patron saint, Nuestra Señora de la Peña (*P*5). This impressive ravine, one of the island's beauty spots, is well worth exploring; see photographs on page 47.

One of the many valleys that sit concealed in the hills surrounding Pájara; this one lies behind Toto (Car tour 1).

Tour 1: There are some unusual carvings on the façade of the church at Pájara — a mixture of Gothic and Aztec decoration. Other examples of Aztec influence are found at La Oliva (see Tour 3).

Now the rest of the valley opens up, and a string of *casas* stretches along it. They're set amidst a healthy sprinkling of palms and cultivated plots — a luxuriant corner (see page 25). The first turn-off you encounter, just before the centre of **Vega de Río de Palmas** (85km) leads down to the reservoir. We continue on the main road by twisting our way up the valley. The countryside subsides into rolling contours once again. Notice a large abandoned field of sisal on the hillsides on your left, a short distance further on. This plant was introduced from Mexico.

At the end of this valley we come to the village of **Betancuria ★** (90km ✝▲✕M; photograph page 26), well hidden from the marauding Berbers of earlier centuries. It's a very picturesque collection of manorial buildings, with a grand 17th-century cathedral. The cathedral and convent here are the oldest examples of their style in the archipelago. Relics abound in historic Betancuria, and I hope you'll notice some of them. A number of the old houses have doorways and arches dating back to the 15th century. Betancuria was the capital of Fuerteventura for some 400 years, up until 1835, and was also the first episcopal seat for all the Canaries. The oldest part of the village huddles around the church — much of it slowly deteriorating. History-hunters will enjoy the cathedral and the small Museo Sacreo here — as well as the municipal museum, when it is finally completed. Everyone passes by the Franciscan monastery, the shell of which sits below the road on the northern side of the village. Inside it (unseen from the rad) are some beautiful cloistered arches (see sketch page 4). Near the convent is a small enclosed church — actually the first church on the island; however much of the building was rebuilt in the 17th century.

Every rural house-hold seems to have its handful of sheep, goats and fowls. All live to-gether in happy harmony.

We zig-zag up out of the valley, and pull over at the top of the pass for a fine panorama over a vast plain to the north. Its far-distant reaches are edged by sharp abrupt hills called *cuchillos* (knives); over on our left lie *morros* (low, smooth hills). Betancuria nestles cosily in the valley floor below. Leaving the viewpoint, we soon pass the turn-off left to Valle de Santa Inés and Llanos de la Concepción (Walk 4). Another expansive plain stretches out below us now, and La Antigua sits below on the edge of it.

Entering **La Antigua** (100km ✝✖), we come to the beautifully laid-out square, with the simple but neverthe-less imposing church. Just north of La Antigua (on the Puerto del Rosario road) stands El Molino ★ (✖), a well preserved 200-year-old windmill, once used for grinding corn. The windmill (*molino*) is an appropriate intro-duction to La Antigua, because this area has the highest concentration of windmills on Fuerteventura — as you will see! From here we head south towards Tuineje.

Out in the country again, palms return to the scene. A trickle of villages is seen sitting back in the plain. Threading our way through hills, we find cultivated fields sheltering along the floors of the *barrancos*. **Agua de Bueyes** (106km ✖) is the next village en route. Three dark volcanoes, La Laguna, Liria and Los Arrabales, rupture the lake of lava that spills out over the plains on your left. This area is called the *malpais* ('badlands'). Around **Tuineje** (112km 🚐) the large *fincas* of the tomato-growers are a prominent feature in a barren landscape.

Coming into **Gran Tarajal** (125km 🏨🚐✖⊕), you look out over lean groves of palms dispersed along the valley floor. Tamarisk (*tarajal*) shrubs add to the verdure. This small port and fishing village is second to Puerto del Rosario (and, to me, much more appealing than the capi-tal). The houses step back up the steep sides of the valley and overlook the black sand beach that curves around the mouth of the *barranco*. Some 6km from Gran Tarajal lies the island's prettiest seaside village, **Las Playitas** (131km ▲✕), terracing a rocky hillock which conceals a lovely dark-sand beach stretching out behind it. Curiosity-seekers may enjoy a detour to El Faro de Entallada.

Homeward bound, return to the GC620 and bear right, then left, for Tarajalejo. (Giniginamar — an optional 8.5km return detour ▲✕ — is a small fishing village, set deep in a *barranco*. To reach it, turn off 6.5km from the Gran Tarajal junction.) **Tarajalejo** (152km ▲▲ ▲✕), once a quiet fishing hamlet, occupies the end of a sweeping beach. Tourism is fast changing all this, as hotels and apartments quickly fill the *barranco* floor. Just over 4km further on, pass a turn-off left for La Lajita, another fishing village all set to capitalise on the tourism boom. We climb amidst low hills, snatching views of pretty coves with not a soul about. Mounting the top of a crest (Cuesta de la Pared, 159km ✕⌨), we have a splendid view of Jandía, encompassing the mountains with the identical twin peaks of Zarza (Walk 7) and Mocán, and the luminous blue and green ribbon of beaches that are the fame of Fuerteventura. Shortly, we rejoin our outgoing route, and I'm sure that this unparalleled coastline will draw you down once more to the beach, before the day is out.

This marooned sailing yacht probably never thought it would end its days as a landmark on the Playa de Sotavento — nor did its owner.

2 PUNTA DE JANDIA AND THE WEST COAST

Morro del Jable • Jandía • Cofete • Morro del Jable
63km/39mi; 3-4 hours driving; Exit B from Morro del Jable
En route: **P** 8, Walk 8

*From beginning to end we follow an exceptionally rough gravel road —
the worst part being the circuit to Cofete. This drive is really only
recommended for four-wheel drive vehicles, especially the Cofete
stretch! Before venturing off in a hired car, read what your rental
agreement says about travelling on* **unsurfaced** *roads. Note that there are
no petrol stations (and hardly any people) out here ... if you break down!
Also, avoid this route after wet weather. This route appeals to the 'rally
drivers' in the population, so drive carefully and attentively, looking out
for speeding traffic. Note also that the peninsula can be very windy, and
that petrol stations are closed on Sundays and holidays.*

As bleak and unfriendly as this landscape may appear,
it is far from unappealing. The wall of ancient
volcanic mountains that dominates the Jandía Peninsula
harbours severe but striking valleys. An air of loneliness
and calm lingers over the plains. Crossing the *cumbre*
from east to west you have spectacular views: the
mountains become more impressive as they sweep back
up into sheer cliffs, the cast beaches more alluring with
their pounding surf. The east coast harbours a number of
secluded coves, the west coast splendid sweeps of sand.
So if you fancy an 'away from it all' beach day, pack a
healthy picnic and make a day of it.

Punta Jandía/Cofete are best reached via the port road,
which circles above Morro del Jable. We turn off just
above the port onto a (signposted) gravel road forking off
to the right. Heading out into one of the most desolate
corners of the island, we bump our way in and out of small
deep *barrancos.* Nearly all of them terminate in pretty
sandy coves — usually accessible only on foot.

Crossing a vast open plain less than five kilometres out,
we pass a fork-off to the right. It heads up into a wide
valley (Gran Valle) that carves a great gap out of the Jandía
massif. This valley offers an alternative route to Cofete —
on foot! This is the old mule track that was the main
east—west link; walk 8 follows it. *Note:* only about 100
metres up the Gran Valle track lies a magnificent
community of rare *Euphorbia handiense* (see opposite).

Sharp rocky ridges dominate the landscape. Low salt-
resistant vegetation — *cosco, aulaga,* ice plants and
Lycium intricatum are the inhabitants of this intractable
terrain. Goats roam deep in the *barrancos.* The large
tomato plantation of **Casas de Jorós** comes as a surprise
way out here in this semi-desert countryside.

Towards the end of the island the plain broadens, and

22

the *barrancos* become less significant. The mountain chain breaks up and slowly subsides into disjointed hills. At Punta de Jandía, the tip of this boot-shaped peninsula, stands the lighthouse. Some 12.5km out of Morro del Jable, we come to the turn-off for Cofete (not signposted). Keeping left, first descend to the lighthouse. Tracks branch off to coves ensconced in the low rocky shoreline running along on the left. Approaching the sleepy fishing hamlet of Puerto de la Cruz, we come onto tarred road, which continues on to the lighthouse (*faro*) 2km further on.

Puerto de la Cruz (21km ✗) seems more like a weekend retreat than a fishing hamlet. Its small adjoining houses sit on the edge of the plain, looking out to sea. **Punta de Jandía** itself is unimpressive; however, you do have a fine view back along the deeply-dissected mountains of the peninsula. Off the point lies an underwater reef called Bajar del Griego ('where the Greek sank'). Some 200 years ago, a Greek ship carrying passengers from Fuerteventura to Gran Canaria hit this reef and sank, with all lives lost.

Tour 2: Only about 100 metres up the Gran Valle track you will see this fine refuge of the rare Euphorbia handiense. Walk 8 follows this old mule track, once the main east—west route across the peninsula.

If you have a four-wheel drive vehicle, now bounce along the track that follows the coast westward, to the pretty rocky cove of Playa de Ojos, some 2km along. Then return to the Cofete turn-off, bear left, and zig-zag up over a pass (📷 with limited parking). Over the *cumbre* a magnificent vista greets you — one of the very best views on the island: you look straight along the golden beaches of Cofete and Barlovento de Jandía. Together they stretch nearly the length of the peninsula. The white-crested breakers and blue-green sea light up the sombre plain and shadowy summits. In the distance rise the billowing sand dunes of the Pared isthmus. Our road, no more than one lane wide, is carved out of the steep face of the escarpment. It was built to enable a certain Señor Winter to construct his mansion out here (see below). Further down the track, you'll spot a large colony of *cande-labra*, a large multi-armed, cactus-like plant ressembling a chandelier. The vil-lagers once used the latex of this plant to catch fish: they put it into rock pools to stun the fish and bring them to the surface.

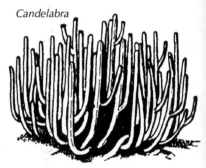

Candelabra

Cofete (40km ✕ *P* 8) is a rustic settlement of stone (and more recently, cement) huts and a restaurant. Its simple low dwellings give it the appearance of a Guanche settlement. Señor Winter, the German who owned the peninsula, forbade anyone to live here, so it never grew into a real village. His villa (see page 58 and sketch page 59) is the main feature of the plain.

Pass through Cofete and bear right. After some 200 metres, you'll meet a track forking off to the left. This leads to a never-ending beach. ***Important:*** the beaches here are dangerous at all times. A cross-current runs just off the shore, and a number of tourists have drowned. Enjoy a picnic, perhaps, and a paddle, but please do not swim! The Winter residence (which no longer belongs to the same family) lies another 1.7km away, should your curiosity get the better of you, but even four-wheel drive vehicles struggle over this stretch of track.

Follow the same route back to Morro del Jable.

3 NORTHERN LANDSCAPES

Corralejo • Puerto del Rosario • La Matilla • Los Molinos •Tindaya • La Oliva • El Cotillo • Corralejo

129km/80mi; under 4 hours driving; Exit A from Corralejo

En route: *P*2; Walks 2, 3

Roads are generally good. Country roads are narrow and occasionally bumpy. Watch out for animals on the roadsides and for pedestrians in the village streets. It can be very windy along the coast. Note that there are petrol stations only in Puerto del Rosario and Corralejo (closed Sundays and holidays).

Barranco de las Peñitas — one of the island's most picturesque valleys (Car tour 1; Picnic 5)

The circuit that this tour follows is fascinating rather than 'beautiful'. Impressive hills and volcanoes border the great interior basins of emptiness. During the second half of the tour you wind in and out of a rough sea of lava called the *malpais* — the 'badlands', a curious sight, with its surprising amount of plant life and greenery. And, if you're bored with the sand dunes of Corralejo, then El Cotillo will prove quite a treat, with its cliff-backed beach and dazzling turquoise coves.

Leave Corralejo on the coastal road to Puerto del Rosario (Exit A) and head out through the dunes. This stunning stretch of white shimmering sand is further enhanced by the aquamarine sea and the purply-blue hills that rise up in the background. Lobos (Walk 1) stands out clearly on your left, offshore, with its hundreds of little hillocks and guardian volcano. The dunes are supposedly a natural park, but all the same, two hotels interrupt this unique stretch of beauty (4.5km 🏔✕).

Tour 1: Betancuria houses a wealth of fine old buildings. This village was the capital of Fuerteventura for some 400 years.

Out of this mini-desert, we cross a featureless stone-littered plain. A number of tourist booklets recommend a detour to Parque Holandés (♠✗), but I would advise you to skip it. **Puerto del Rosario** (30km ♠♠♠✗✝➍⊕) has little to offer, being visibly the poorest town on the island. However, at Hostal Macario you'll find good home-cooking.

Beyond Puerto del Rosario, our tour really begins, as we head back northwest to Corralejo via the inland route*. Head straight out of town on Calle León y Castillo (on the right-hand side of the church, Exit B). This takes you onto the GC600. A gentle ascent across a stony plain brings us up to the old airport of Los Estancos, and we cut straight through the centre of it. Entering a grand U-shaped valley, we pass through **Tetir** (38km), a well-spread farming village. The enclosing hills are eroded and rocky, bare of vegetation. Montaña Aceitunal (686m/2250ft) dominates the valley with its sharply-pointed features. Climbing out of this valley, we reach a higher one and come onto the pretty village of **La Matilla** (43km). Another prominent mountain of equal proportions overshadows the village: Montaña Muda (689m/2260ft).

Descending from this basin meet a junction at 45km and bear left. **Tefía** (51km), a sad, forgotten-looking village of decaying stone buildings, sits quite lost in this quiet corner. We turn off down the first road forking off to the right beyond Tefía (signposted for Puertito de los Molinos). Wine-coloured *cosco* patches the arid flat. Pass through the village of **Colonia García Escámez**, a farming settlement built after the construction of the nearby (but out of sight) Embalse de los Molinos. Walk 4 takes you to this *embalse* (reservoir; see photograph page 44). Dip down into the Barranco de los Molinos. It's a pretty valley to explore (downstream), especially after a wet winter, when you'll find a stream and some rock pools. **Los Molinos** (62km) is a tiny fishing hamlet that huddles off a lovely bay encircled by the rock cliffs that open off the mouth of the *barranco*.

Return to the junction below La Matilla and bear left for Corralejo. Rounding a corner, we look over onto the dark sandy volcano of Montaña Quemada. This particular

*An alternative route back to Corralejo lies further south and would take you via El Castillo (▮♠♠✗). I don't think this itinerary is worth the extra kilometres. However, if you're making a trip to Jandía, either go or return via this route to see the enormous U-shaped valleys beyond El Castillo. Visit, too, Pozo Negro (♠✗), an out-of-the-way fishing village sprinkled across a lava tongue — a 17km (return) detour.

volcano is rather special because at its base there is a modest monument dedicated to the famous Spanish poet Unamuno, who lived in exile on Fuerteventura.

We next pass above **Tindaya** (81km ✕). It spreads across a flattened crest amidst a profusion of faded brown stone walls. Behind the village stands captivating Montaña Tindaya (the setting for Walk 3), a great rocky salient that dominates the surrounding countryside with its boldness (see photograph page 38). Perhaps this is why the Guanches chose it as their holy mountain.

At the other end of this plain lies the pleasant country village of **La Oliva** ★ (87km ☗✕). It rests on the edge of a lava flow. Montaña Arena, a mountain of sand, rises up out of the lava flow in the background. La Oliva was a town of some importance in the 17th century, when the island's military post was stationed here. The official residence (the colonels' house; sketch page 6) can be seen abandoned on the outskirts of the village, on your right, as you enter. A curious feature of the house is that it contains 365 doors and windows. To the left of the building stand the rustic servants' quarters and stables. One can't help but notice the perfectly-shaped Montaña Frontón rising up in the background of this naked setting; in fact, it's not a real mountain, but only the tail of a long ridge. The parish church at La Oliva, Nuestra Señora de Candelaria, overpowers the village with its solid black-stone belfry. The Casa del Capellán (chaplain's house), another old and dilapidated building, sits off the side of the Corralejo road, on the left. This house, and a small house in the village, which has a stone façade with an Aztec motif, are other examples of the as yet unexplained Mexican influence (see also Tour 1, Pájara).

From La Oliva you can take an alternative route home another day, via Caldereta: head east for the coast and keep left at the first junction (see the touring map). This quiet little village has some excellent examples of traditional architecture, from simple farm dwellings to comfortable villas. But today's tour leaves La Oliva for Lajares: take the road forking off left opposite the church (not signposted). The road runs alongside the pale green lichen-smeared *malpais* (the 'badlands') — a pleasant change in the landscape. We circle Montaña La Arena before coming into **Lajares** (96km) and passing between two roadside windmills. The one on our left is called a *molina*: a wooden contraption that rotates and is built onto the rooftop of a house. The house normally has a room on either side of the mill. On our right we have a *molino*: it's conical and is moved by pushing the long arms, thus moving the cap with the windmill blades. This building is not inhabited. Both mills were used for grinding *gofio*. See sketches on pages 1 and 2. Lajares is an attractive little village of white houses set amidst dark lava-stone walls.

We follow the lava flow all the way to **El Cotillo** (103km ▲✕), at present just a jumble of houses set around a pretty rocky port. Make the most of it now; the speculators have found another stupendous stretch of coast to develop. A superb beach set below cliffs lies over to the left of the village. Take any of the tracks leading out past the 17th-century watchtower — Castillo de Rico Roque (■), perched on the cliffs at the edge of the village. You will find exquisite little coves ensconced in the dark lava coastline (***Picnic 2***; photograph page 37).

When you call it a day, the homeward-bound route is straightforward. Keep straight on (left) through Lajares and, at the GC600, keep left for Corralejo.

In spring patches of scarlet poppies light up the countryside. The windmill in the background is used for drawing water from sunken wells (see notes on page 16).

1 AROUND LOBOS

Distance: 10km/6.2mi; 1h45min

Grade: easy, but there is no shade, and it can be hot, windy and dusty.

Equipment: comfortable shoes, cardigan, sunhat, suncream, picnic, plenty of water, swimwear

How to get there: 🛥 from Corralejo to Lobos
Departs Corralejo at 10.00 daily
To return: same 🛥 from Lobos; departs 16.00 daily

You can have Jandía and El Jable; I'll settle for Lobos any day. A 35-minute — and not too rough — ferry ride with an amiable seafarer takes you over to this strange little island of sand and rocky mounds. Seen from Corralejo, it may not even arouse your curiosity. But once you've seen the exquisite lagoon cradled by Casas El Puertito and you've climbed the crater, then finished your day with a dip in the turquoise green waters off the shore, you'll remember it as one of the most beautiful spots on Fuerteventura. Lobos takes its name from the seals that once inhabited these waters. The island is only 3km off the coast of Fuerteventura and measures 6.5km square.

We follow a track that circles the island. No one lives on Lobos, so there are no vehicles. Straight off the jetty **start out** by taking the right-hand fork and head for the tiny port of Casas El Puertito, a few minutes away. A neat wide path leads us through a landscape dominated by mounds of lava and littered with rock. These small mounds, called *hornitos* ('little ovens'; see page 32) are caused by phreatic eruptions. You'll see the very beautiful *Limonium papillatum*, with its paper-like mauve and white flowers. And fluorescent green *tabaiba* glows amidst the sombre rock. You'll also notice plenty of *cosco* (*Launaea arborescens*; see page 40), a noticeably bright reddish plant, and *suaeda* (*Polygonum maritimum*).

A reef of rocky outcrops shelters the lagoon, making it into a perfect natural swimming pool. Through the rock you can see the sand dunes of Corralejo in the background; this is a picture postcard setting. Exiting from the little houses, we continue around the lagoon. Almost at once, swing back inland and come to a T-junction: keep left here. *Arthrocnemum fruticosum* (a fern-like plant) grows in the hollows. Ice plants, with their transparent papillae resembling drops of water, may also catch your attention. This plant was once traded for its soda content. The track loops its way through these miniature 'mountains'. Small sandy depressions lie ensconced amidst them. The rock is clad in orange and faded-green

LOBOS

aleta del Palo

Lobos
127
Caldera de la Montaña

Playa de la Calera

Punta Martino
Faro de Lobos

Casas el Puertito

Caleta de la Rasca

lichen. Overlooking all this is Montaña Lobos (the crater), the most prominent feature in this natural park.

Shortly, cross a sandy flat area. The track forks; the right-hand fork becomes a path and cuts off a couple of corners and rejoins the main route on the top of a bank. Lanzarote begins to grow across the horizon. Ignore the forks off to the right at **15min** and **20min** into the walk. The second fork leads past a patch of *sisal* — an aloe-like plant with exceptionally tall flower stems, sheltering in a hollow just two minutes away. Close on **30min** into the walk, you come to a faint T-junction. Bear left and, minutes further along, join a track from the left, just below the lighthouse. Then climb up to it on a paved way. In two minutes you're alongside the abandoned building and its outhouses. If you don't intend to climb the crater, this will be your best viewpoint in the walk. You look out over the dark lava hills and the tiny valleys of golden sand that thread their way through them. To the right of the broken-away crater of Montaña Lobos you'll glimpse Corralejo. Across the straight lie Lanzarote's magnificent beaches, stretching from Playa Blanca to Punta Papagayo (just opposite you).

From the lighthouse we follow the main track off to the right, into a manicured landscape. Just over fifteen minutes from the lighthouse (at about **55min**), we turn off to climb Montaña Lobos. Take the first (faint) fork-off you come to, on your right. Straight into this track, the route forks. Go right and, some 115 paces along this fading fork, head straight off across the stones, aiming for the path that ascends the crater. Within two minutes, cross a sandy hollow and reach the rim of the crater at about **1h05min.**

A brilliant sight awaits you. You find yourself on a razor-sharp ridge, looking down sheer walls onto a beach, hidden inside this half-crater. Your vista encompasses the profusion of *hornitos* that make up this island, the dunes of Corralejo, and the hazy inland hills. To the north, you can see all along the coastline of Lanzarote, as far as Puerto del Carmen.

Returning to the main track, head right. Barely ten minutes after joining the track, we pass behind the beach without noticing it. The turn-off to the beach lies two minutes beyond a fisherman's cottage that sits in a hollow on your left. The exquisite bay is actually a shallow lagoon that curves back deeply into the coastline. Here's where you'll end up passing the rest of the day, no doubt. Don't forget that the boat leaves at 4pm! To return to the ferry, just continue along the track.

The 'hornitos' of Lobos — an intriguing landscape

2 EL COTILLO • CASAS DE MAJANICHO • CORRALEJO

Distance: 22km/13.5mi; 3h45min

Grade: easy but long. Note that it can be *very* hot; also windy and dusty.

Equipment: comfortable shoes, cardigan, sunhat, suncream, raingear, swimwear, picnic, pleny of water

How to get there: 🚐 from Puerto del Rosario to El Cotillo (via Corralejo)

To return: taxi from Corralejo to Puerto del Rosario (or bus on the *following* day, if you spend the night at Corralejo)

Short walk: El Cotillo—Cortijo de la Costilla—El Cotillo: easy; 2h30min. Take bus as main walk; return by taxi. You can shorten this walk by another 30 minutes if you have a car: Drive almost as far as the lighthouse and leave your vehicle by the turn-off point (alongside an old water cistern on your right). However, due to the number of car break-ins, it would be wiser to leave it in the village or at one of the more popular coves en route.

Beyond the ramshackle fishing village of El Cotillo you pass superb little *playas* — white sand coves and limpid turquoise waters embraced by dark jagged arms of lava. With civilisation behind you, you head into a no-man's land, crossing a vast sea-plain and at times floundering through dunes or through rough seas of lava. Wherever you look, there are stones and rock and plains stretching for miles in all directions. But just when you're getting tired, another alluring cove appears. Time this hike for the early afternoon, when you can take dips in the numerous coves at the start of the walk and cross the inhospitable sea-plain in the cool of the evening.*

Leave the bus just inside El Cotillo, outside Supermercado El Cotillo. **Start out** by walking a few metres back to the gravel road the bus has just turned off, and bear left along it, making

*Note: The entire course of this walk can be done in a jeep, since it follows a track. But don't attempt it in your rented *car*; it's very rough in places. Remember the wording of your car-hire contract: no venturing off sealed roads is covered by insurance! *Note also:* A highly recommended bicycle excursion of 28km follows the route Corralejo—Casas de Majanicho—Lajares—Corralejo. The first 8.5km is on a bumpy dirt track. Avoid cycling on windy days! Cycles are available for rent in Corralejo.

33

N

0   2km

1mi

Copyright © Sunflower Books

Caleta de Beatriz

Caleta de Punta Aguada

Punta de Tostón
Faro de Tostón

P

Playa de Marfolin

Urbanización
Los Lagos

Corralejos

COTILLO

■ **Castillo de Rico Roque**

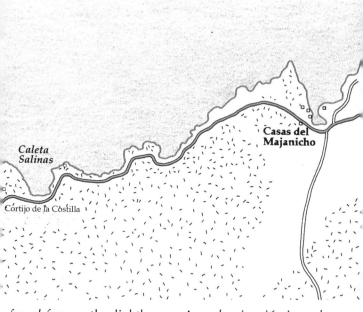

for *el faro* — the lighthouse. An *urbanización* is under way on the outskirts of El Cotillo, so the description of the first kilometre or two of this walk may change by the time you use the book. Keep straight through the new housing development, crossing a flat and sandy landscape. The way continues to the lighthouse (Faro de Tostón). Some tempting coves come out of hiding. Can you resist them? The vivid colours of the sea, the sand, and the lava around here could sell anyone on a Fuerteventura holiday.

It's quite on the cards that you will be walking into a strong wind. Reefs of rock shelter small lagoons. The red-and white-striped lighthouse is the only landmark in this flat countryside. Inland, however, high hills run along the horizon. The salt-white dunes glare in the sun.

At about **30min** into the walk, not long before reaching the lighthouse, we turn off the road onto a faint sandy track veering off right. An old water cistern marks the spot. Before you lies an alluring seascape of bright coves snuggled into the jagged shore, with warm white dunes rolling back off them. These little beaches are never crowded.

Some fifteen minutes off the road we join a track coming from the right, to discover *malpais* ('badland') lava creeping in on us. This 'AA'-type lava is speckled with orange and grey-green lichen. Rock layers the ground, leaving not even a breathing space. The sand is sprinkled

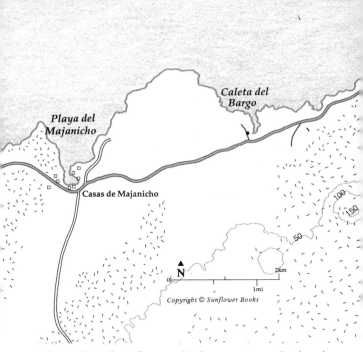

with small yellow flowers (*Tabaceae ononis*). Shortly we pass through a stone wall that fences off the dunes and cross a corner of the *malpais*. Ignore the faint fork-off left immediately through the wall. (You will remain on the main track all the way to Corralejo.) Dropping into a dusty flat, the track branches off in all directions. Head across towards the sea, bearing right, and pick up the track again as it re-enters the sand.

Looking across the *malpais* one is surprised to find that it is all fenced off by walls and well clothed in greenery. At the **1h15min**-mark we mount a gentle rise to find a fishermen's outpost consisting of a few sheds and houses — Cortijo de la Costilla. It rests on the edge of the lava, around an inlet. One of the little houses even sports a television aerial! On hazeless days you can see Lanzarote just across the straights. Midway along the track swings inland and, further along the coast, dozens of windsurfers can be seen zipping across the sea. Gradually Casas de Majanicho introduces itself. This collection of beach shacks and a couple of houses is plonked around another deeply-set inlet. The windsurfing takes place to the right of this settlement — it's one of the 'in' places.

At just over **2h** en route come to a junction, behind the houses. Continue straight on. (A right turn would take you out onto the main Cotillo road.) The way now becomes an earthen track/road. Playa Blanca is the splash of white

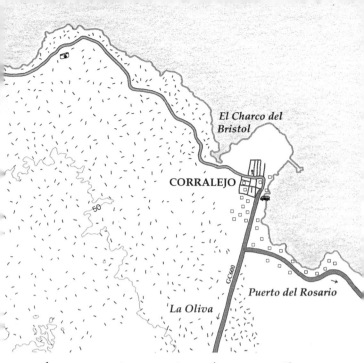

across from you, on Lanzarote's southern coast. Closer to Corralejo, the 'pimply' islet of Lobos (Walk 1) comes into sight, with its prominent crater sharply outlined. At **3h30min** we enter Corralejo from the rear, join a track coming in from the right, and head straight down (notice the old windmill here on your left) into the resort. Minutes down, swing up right to the centre. If you're staying the night here, you'll find your bus tomorrow outside the Centro Atlántico; it leaves for Puerto del Rosario at 07.30 (weekdays) or 07.45 (Sundays).

Setting off across the dunes, we look back onto the Faro de Tostón.

3 MONTAÑA TINDAYA

Distance: 6km/3.8mi; 1h15min

Grade: a strenuous, but short, ascent of 220m/720ft up a very steep, rocky mountain. This hike is difficult for inexperienced walkers and would be dangerous in wet weather.

Equipment: walking boots with good grip and ankle support, cardigan, sunhat, suncream, raingear, picnic, plenty of water

How to get there: Corralejo-🚌 or Puerto del Rosario-🚌 to Tindaya; alight at the junction above the village.

To return: 🚌 from Tindaya to Corralejo, or taxi to Puerto del Rosario (arrange for a taxi beforehand, or telephone from the restaurant below the junction).

Montaña Tindaya is no ordinary mountain. Not only is it a prominent feature in the landscape, but the Guanches regarded it as their holy mountain. On its summit they slaughtered young goats and offered these sacrifices to their gods. A number of important relics from the Guanche epoch have been found on the mountain, and rock engravings such as those on page 40 can still be seen around the summit.

Barley fields sprinkled with poppies encircle Montaña Tindaya (Walk 3, Car tour 3).

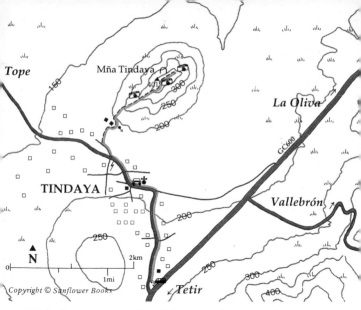

Off the bus, **start out** by following the road down into the village. Go to the church square (also the best place to leave a hired car). This peaceful farming settlement curves around the gentle slopes of a sprawling hill. The houses are scattered amidst garden plots, which sit behind the tired stone walls criss-crossing the inclines. Goats and sheep doze in their pens. Here on Fuerteventura the goats are quite a breed. Some nannies are able to give as many as 8 litres of milk over a 24-hour period! Past the church, the road curves around to the right. Now Montaña Tindaya stands before you; its sheer inclines make the summit appear inaccessible.

Five minutes beyond the church (some 60m/yds along from an electricity transformer station on your left), a small farm track forks off to the right. Take it but, a minute in, fork off onto a fainter track ascending to the right, into fields of barley. When the track fizzles out a minute further on, head up to the two derelict stone cottages in front of you (at the base of the hill). Your ascent begins just behind them, where you climb the tail of the ridge. The ground is stony and carpeted in wine-coloured *cosco* (see page 40) and ice plants. When food was scarce in years gone by, the dried fruit of the *cosco* plant was used to make an ersatz *gofio* (an important food source on the island, usually made from roasted corn). The fallen fruit of the *cosco* was collected and ground into powder.

Your way up is very straightforward: stick to the top of the crest all the way. Above the gravel you come onto bare rock. In places you'll be down on all fours.

At about **40min** you reach the summit. (The crest topples off onto the plains below some three to four minutes further on, so take care!) You have a fine view of the surrounding countryside. On clear days you can see Lanzarote — El Cotillo is the village ensconced in the coastline over on the left, and La Oliva is the sprinkling of white straight ahead off the end of the mountain. Immediately below, on the left-hand side of the mountain, sits a picturesque homestead surrounded by gardens and a lean palm grove — a pretty picture in this harsh landscape. Two minutes beyond the summit, notice the cave-like shelter set in the hillside just below on your left. This is a good place to seek shade if you've the courage to slide down the mountain face and you don't mind an enormous boulder sitting over your head....

Now for the treasure hunt. Most of the drawings/engravings are around the summit. The easiest to find are the two on an upright, smooth rock face just below the summit (on the eastern, or village side). The engravings are within a radius of some 5 to 8 metres (15 to 25 feet) from the top of the peak. Others are located on the next clump of rock further along the ridge. Once you've found one, you soon find the others. The diagrams help you to identify them. *Suerte!*

Descending the mountain is slow going. A lot of care is needed. Allow yourself enough time to return to the bus, if you didn't come by car.

A herdsman watering his goats at a small tank near the base of Montaña Tindaya. Notice the deep red cosco in the foreground.

Distance: 13km/8mi; 2h15min

Grade: moderate. Much of the walk is freewheeling over stony terrain. It can be very hot, and there is no shade beyond the reservoir.

Equipment: walking boots or stout shoes with ankle support, cardigan, sunhat, suncream, raingear, picnic, plenty of water

How to get there and return: only accessible by private transport

The Embalse de los Molinos is the largest reservoir on Fuerteventura. Its water level varies from year to year. Seeing a body of water in this dry and barren landscape is indeed a strange sight and, from the hilltops above, it makes quite a picture. Heading home, you mingle with goats and sheep, as you traipse over rolling ridges with grand views over this desolate countryside.

Leave your transport outside Bar García in Llanos de la Concepción. **Setting out**, take the track that runs down into the village from the bar. This scattering of houses is deep in slumber. Most of the garden plots are untended and overgrown. The walls no longer stand proud and straight. Notice the earthen oven on the left-hand side of the track a couple of minutes down. Clumps of prickly-pear and a few thick-leafed aloes sit behind the tired walls. Pass through an intersection and, two minutes further on, when the track forks (outside a shop), keep straight on — to the right. Another track joins you from the left a few minutes later. This is followed by a streambed crossing.

We head across a vast valley, its left side lined by smooth worn hills and its right side bordered by *cuchillos* (Spanish for 'knives': these are younger and sharper hills). The terrain is stony and dry. Solitary cultivated corners make a sharp contrast in this ochre-coloured landscape, with their vivid greenery. In spring scarlet poppies and daisies run amok in the gardens, and the plain is smeared with the cereal-like *Gramineae*. Within **15min** pass through another intersection, keeping straight on. A few lone houses seek solitude in this great expanse of open country.

Approaching the **30min**-mark we again re-enter the streambed, just as it joins another from the right. Metres (yards) along we leave it and the main track as well, ascending a faint fork-off to the left. An abandoned farmstead lies up ahead. The *barranco* begins folding up, and it's still dry. When the way swings up to the farmhouse, you continue straight off it, following the

41

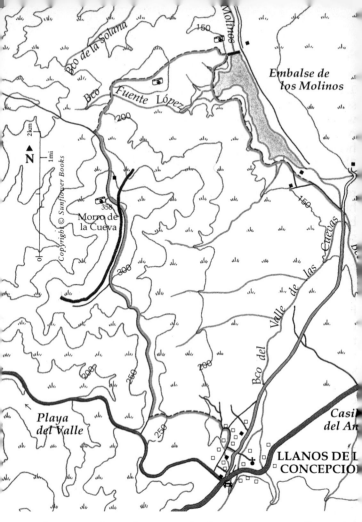

barranco. Soon the streambed opens up, revealing a rive
of tamarisk shrubs — the only shrubs in this countryside
They shelter here along the damp valley floor. Briefly joi
a two-wheeled track and cross through a dense colony o
ice plants and *cosco.* You catch sight of the dam wall u
ahead and gradually the tail of water below grows into
good-sized muddy brown reservoir. If you're int
ornithology, go quietly: birds do congregate around th
muddy end of the dam here. These tamarisk offer the onl
shade you'll find on the route of this walk, so it's a goo
picnic spot on a hot day … if you'll pardon the flies.

Continuing around the *presa,* you'll need to scrambl
up the rocky slopes and make your way around th
inclines above the reservoir — one of the most attractiv
spots on the walk, where *Asphodelus* covers the slope

An arm of water in a small side-*barranco* needs skirting. This is also a good spot for bird-watching, and you may spot some herons. Keep around the edge of the arm of water and then ascend the side of the ridge. Descending onto the wall of the dam needs careful footwork; the hillside is steep and gravelly. You reach the wall at about **1h**. From there scramble up onto the top of the crest above the dam: from here you'll have a good vista over the reservoir and across the valley to the impressive barrier of hills. A small village (Colonia García Escamez) of white block houses lies near the end of the valley. Red *cosco* stains the surrounding inclines, and a hint of green lies in the sheltered folds. The serenity and isolation of this landscape has a beauty all its own.

Home is now over the hills we've just circled. Landmarks to aim for are (with your back to the reservoir): the hilltop immediately above, from where you curve round to the hills over on your left — heading for the stone wall that crosses over them. The timing of this leg of the walk will depend on how quickly you want to reach that summit. Once you've come to the first hilltop, descend briefly to your right, before crossing the streambed below on your left. The beauty of freewheeling on these low hills is that it's just about impossible to get lost.

At about **1h20min** cross the streambed that runs between the two ridges. Mounting an adjoining ridge, you come onto a faint two-wheeled track and look straight out over another valley. Pass a stone shelter near the top of the crest and soon the coast comes into view on your right. Close on **1h40min** into the walk you reach the second hilltop (Morro de la Cueva) and the highest point in the walk (363m/1190ft) — near the 'Great Wall' of Llanos de la Concepción (an impressive stretch of wall along the top of the ridge). On these slopes you'll encounter a rather comical-looking flock of sheep grazing. Inland lie bare desiccated hills, climbing one upon the other.

Remaining on the track, pass through the wall and follow it all along the top of the ridge. Llanos de la Concepción is now in sight below you. Valle de Santa Inés huddles high in the hills. Ten minutes through the walls, our track swings up onto a lateral ridge branching off left (towards the village). The wall and a faint fork continue to the right. More of Santa Inés opens up, and terracing, stepping shallow *barrancos*, comes out of hiding.

Descending to the village, we pass by two rubbish dumps (hopefully the expected upsurge in tourism to the

Embalse de los Molinos, Fuerteventura's largest reservoir — and a good spot for bird-watching. The surrounding countryside is silent and barren.

island will elicit some action on the part of the government to get rid of Fuerteventura's many unsightly rubbish dumps…). Just past the second dump, some fifteen minutes down (not far off a road), leave the track and descend to the village on a goats' path. Rounding the crest, our path quickly fades out. Then we flounder over loose stones and gravel, before coming into the village.

Descending the hill, keep the church on your left and find a farm track at the bottom of the stone wall that runs down on your right. Follow this track to a gravel driveway. Almost immediately you'll join a track from the left and, two minutes later, take the first turn-off left. This takes you down onto the track you set off along at the start of the walk — the intersection above the church. Bear right and, in three minutes, at **2h15min**, you're back at the bar (open from 5.30 or 6.00 pm) all ready for a beer….

5 BARRANCO DE LAS PEÑITAS (VEGA DE RIO DE PALMAS)

Distance: 5km/3mi; 1h30min   **See also photograph page 25**

Grade: quite easy, but the path to the chapel could prove unnerving for those prone to vertigo. Be very careful if it's wet!

Equipment: comfortable shoes or walking boots, cardigan, sunhat, suncream, raingear, picnic, plenty of water

How to get there and return: only accessible by private transport

This stroll is short and sweet; it takes us down one of the island's most picturesque valleys, the Barranco de las Peñitas. Palm trees dot the valley, and a small reservoir rests in the floor. From the reservoir wall you look through a corridor of rock out onto more palms and salubrious garden plots far below. In winter you may find dark green pools embedded in the floor of the *barranco*. Hidden in the sheer walls lies the delightful little Ermita de Nuestra Señora de la Peña — just the kind of place where one might feel inclined to offer up a prayer.

To reach the **starting point** of the walk, turn off the GC620 (approaching from Pajara) just before the centre of Vega de Río de Palmas and drive down towards the reservoir. The safest place to leave your car is probably just past the school building, half a kilometre downhill, on your left. For the first five minutes of the walk we follow the road, passing the last of the houses. A healthy sprinkling of tall palms graces the valley floor and indeed, the entire valley. For Fuerteventura, this is the height of arboreal luxury! Abrupt craggy ridges dominate the landscape.

We turn off from the road onto a wide goats' path; this heads off to the right, just before a culvert and bridge. The goats' path follows the streambed. A minute along we drop down into it (just to the right of a stone embankment crossing the *barranco*). Some ten minutes below the bridge (**15min**) we come to clumps of tamarisk in the middle of the streambed. Here we climb out of the *barranco* onto an old washed-out track that ascends to the right. The valley floor quickly fills with tamarisk and then forks. The left-hand fork swings back up into the hills;

the right-hand fork cradles the reservoir, before folding up into a narrow ravine that drops down to join the Barranco de Mal Paso.

We're surrounded by hills. The pointed Gran Montaña (708m/2320ft) dominates the valley. Soon the murky green *presa* is just below you. Green garden plots set amidst palm trees terrace the slopes on your left now. Our *barranco*, barren and bouldery, is freckled with *verod* — the brightest plant on the slopes. Five minutes along the track ends, directly above the reservoir wall. The bare escarpment stares down on us, as it closes up into a deep 'V' which empties out onto an oasis of palms and gardens before continuing its seaward journey. If you want to see more of this scenic *barranco*, head back up the track for a minute, or until you can scramble down the hillside (without ending up in the reservoir!) to the goats' path that runs along the water's edge, and head along this to the reservoir wall. Take care — it's a bit narrow!

Beyond the reservoir wall we follow a stone-paved path that has been built into the sides of the *barranco*. Parts of this path are tricky going, where it has crumbled away ... and the lizards darting every which way don't help. The pools may be no more than puddles by the time you use this book, but they *can* be very deep. A few minutes down the path you spot the tiny white chapel of Nuestra Señora de la Peña perched on a rocky outcrop above the streambed. We turn

off to the chapel a minute later. This path clings to the face of the rock and is quite unnerving, but it's fairly short — only some 30m/yds. Inside the chapel you'll find a 15th-century alabaster image of the island's patron saint, Our Lady of the Rock, as well as a visitor's book that makes for interesting reading. On a scorchingly-hot day, the chapel provides the perfect retreat for a picnic. Beyond the *ermita* the path hangs out over the side of the *barranco*. This stretch of path might also prove unnerving for those without a head for heights. It's

The tiny chapel of Nuestra Señora de la Peña is well concealed in a sheer ravine. Can you spot it? There's a close-up view below. Another photo of this lovely barranco is on page 25 (Picnic 5, Car tour 1).

an impressive piece of path-building, that's for certain. Nearing the end of the *barranco*, a few minutes along, the path vanishes. We call it quits here, **40min** after setting out. This is a very picturesque corner of the valley, where you look out over gardens and the on-going ravine.

Returning, we follow the same route but, instead of climbing to the track above the reservoir, we remain on the goats' path, keeping around the hillside until we re-enter the streambed just above the reservoir. There's quite a bit of bird life near the water's edge; keep your eyes peeled!

Picnic 5: The chapel of Nuestra Señora de la Peña in the Peñitas barranco. Fine pools like these are a rarity on Fuerteventura!

6 PUERTO DE LA PEÑA • BARRANCO DE LA MADRE DEL AGUA • PEÑA HORADADA • PUERTO DE LA PEÑA

Distance: 12km/7.5mi; 2h15min

Grade: moderate. The beginning of the walk is awkward and involves some scrambling; however, it is not difficult. The ascent in the rocky bed of the Barranco de la Madre del Agua will be slow. Getting into the cave at the end of the hike requires sure-footedness and a head for heights, and should only be attempted by very experienced walkers. Don't attempt this hike in wet weather.

Equipment: comfortable shoes or walking boots, cardigan, sunhat, raingear, suncream, swimwear, picnic, plenty of water

How to get there and return: accessible by private transport only

Short walks: both are easy —
1 Puerto de la Peña—Peña Horadada—Puerto de la Peña (1h10min). Do the walk in reverse by using the notes for Picnic 6b as far as the Caleta Negra overlook; then refer to the map to continue to the Peña Horadada. Wear comfortable shoes and take swimming things. *Note:* Swim in the pool below the rock with the hole in it (see below); the beach looks potentially dangerous to me.
2 Puerto de la Peña—Barranco de la Madre del Agua—Puerto de la Peña (45min). Follow the main walk as far as Barranco de la Madre del Agua. If it appeals to you, do some exploring there.

This excursion gives you a taste of everything. It's well worth a day of your holiday. You set out seeing some of Fuerteventura's loveliest palm groves and then ascend a tiny *barranco* unique for its permanent flowing stream (don't expect a torrent, however!). Set out early in the morning, so you can see the goatherds milking their goats at a corral midway into the walk. Later in the day, we enjoy some striking coastal scenery, as we detour to the rock with a hole in it and the caves of Caleta Negra.

This monumental rock with a hole in it ('Peña Horadada') sits at the mouth of the Barranco de la Peña. The small pool beneath it is ideal for cooling off....

The usual problem is, where to leave the car? The safest place (but not the closest) is Puerto de la Peña, from where you can walk back up the road for ten minutes and then **begin the walk.** Just beyond an abandoned homestead across the *barranco*, see a faint track forking off the road to it, crossing a garden plot, and descending into the *barranco*. Follow this track. We head up this wide stream-bed to the right, along the track. A profusion of tamarisk trees grows along the sides of the banks; they soon broaden out into hedges and create windbreaks for the gardens. Approaching our turn-off, we pass small groves of tall palms.

The Barranco de la Madre del Agua is a discrete narrow ravine that slices its way into the ridge trailing down on our left. Palm trees peeping out of it give its presence away. A small farm sits opposite it. Less than ten minutes up the *barranco*, when the track veers off along the right-hand side of the streambed, we continue over to the left, to Madre del Agua. The initial stretch of this ravine is the most awkward part of the hike, since we have to flounder over rocks and palm fronds (watch out for these!) in the streambed. As compensation, this cool shady grove is a delightful discovery, with its murmuring little stream and clear pools. A neat stone wall lining the right-hand bank, and a charming crumbled stone bridge catch your attention through the trees (see page 51). Further ahead, the ravine floor is choked with cane. Altogether, it's a pleasant place to explore, especially on a hot day.

Once you've done some exploring, the easiest way out is to cross the bridge and ascend the right-hand wall of the ravine, scaling above a small tank just beyond the bridge. Follow the goats' path along the steep gravelly hillside, keeping above the cane. Past the cane, you re-enter the streambed just by an old and twisted tamarisk tree (five minutes from the bridge). The jungle of vegetation has vanished, and we now scramble up the rocky ravine floor. The walls rise straight up above us. Depending on the rains, small *charcos* (pools) lie at intervals; beyond the cane the stream is subterranean and only occasionally resurfaces. A couple of pools may require tricky footwork. *Asphodelus* and the stringy tobacco plant shrub (*Nicotiana glauca*) are the sole survivors up here. It's a most inhospitable landscape, where only goats can forage. Still, you may see some birds up here.

Some **25min** of twisting and turning brings you to a small *barranco* forking off left from the main ravine. An old stone wall climbs out of the streambed to the left just at this point. Here we also scramble out of the streambed and ascend to the crest above; this is easiest done by climbing the left-hand side of the *barranco*. Three minutes up (at about **50min** into the walk) we find ourselves on the well-rounded top of a crest, where we find a faint track. Half a minute across the crest, we look down into a much grander *barranco* — the Barranco de la Peña, which may also carry a trickle of water. Smooth, rounded hills, bare of life, grow up in the background.

At the mouth of the Barranco de la Madre del Agua — the site of a permanently-flowing stream. Here you can enjoy Picnic 6a, under a profusion of palms.

Continuing down the stony track, pass the crumbled remains of an old corral. In the distance, to the left, you can see the village of Mezguez, noticeable for its grassy surroundings. At just over **1h** you pass (quietly, please) a large corral. This is the home of a handsome herd of goats and a number of sheep. The animals are milked in the morning, then turned out to graze. Please note — the family here is reserved and not used to intruders. So don't interrupt their privacy, unless they invite you over, and do ask for permission before taking any photographs ("Por favor" — pointing to your camera). Watching the herd at play is very amusing. The dogs are noisy and harmless.

From the corral you follow a clear track downhill. The coast begins to appear, and you catch a glimpse of Puerto de la Peña, a small gathering of modest houses set back off the sea. Twenty minutes below the corral come to a junction. Keep right. A minute along, pass a fork-off left: this is your return route. Dipping to the sea, the majestic Peña Horadada (the 'rock with a hole in it') dramatically appears. This massive 'Arc de Triomphe' of rock thrusts up off the beach at the water's edge. We descend now into the Barranco de la Peña, over which we looked earlier.

Close on **1h35min** you're standing below the great gaping hole, dwarfed by this monumental wall of rock. A splendid little pool, which the waves replenish, sits below the hole. The coastline is wild and very beautiful. If you plan to swim, please use the pool; the beach is dangerous.

We follow the same track out, but turn off it some ten minutes along. Take the faint fork to the right (mentioned earlier) that heads towards the top of the cliffs. Minutes along, when the way ends, bear left and, a minute later, you're on the edge of the cliffs with a magnificent view around Caleta Negra. The caves you see cutting back into the walls over on the left can be reached by following the steps down to the old pier. Three minutes around the cliffs bring you to the descending point (steps). *Note: this descent is only recommended for very experienced and sure-footed walkers; you'll have to scramble some 2m/6ft down to the steps (the top steps are washed away) — on all fours, and with the sea thrashing around directly below you. Don't venture down to the caves if the sea is rough!* A goats' path leads down to the steps, which are to the left of the stone wall lodged in the face of the hill just below the top of the crest. Two minutes down, you're overlooking the pier and a minute later you're on the sandy floor of the first massive cavern. Another, narrower cave reaches to within 50 metres/yards of Puerto de la Peña! But please — just take my word for it and remain in the main chamber. Don't go exploring!

Now making for Puerto de la Peña, continue around the top of the crest and in two minutes overlook the village and its black sand beach. Head along the crest to the point on your right and scramble down to the old path to the pier. Follow it into the village(**2h10min**).

7 PICO DE LA ZARZA

Distance: 16km/10mi; 3h15min   **Photograph opposite**

Grade: strenuous, with an ascent of 807m/2650ft. The first 75 minutes of the walk follows a track, but then you must clamber over rocks and stones for about 20 minutes more to reach the summit. It can be very hot — or very cold and windy. Not recommended on very windy days — nor on cloudy days, since the climb is only worth it for the view and, if you were lost in mist, the climb could be dangerous as well. But everyone who is fit should try this hike, beginners included.

Equipment: walking boots or stout shoes with ankle support, warm jacket, raingear, sunhat (and something with which to tie it to your head!), suncream, picnic, plenty of water

How to get there and return: with your own rented car, or by taxi to the Hotel Río Ventura in the Barranco de Vinamar

P ico de la Zarza is Fuerteventura's highest peak and worth climbing for two reasons: the grand panorama that tumbles away below you and the wealth of botanical specimens to be seen en route. The best time to scale this mountain is in spring, when the summit is resplendent with yellow-flowering *Asteriscus* (see opposite). But, be warned: it can be *very* windy! On a calm day, it's one of the most exhilarating spots on the island.

The **departing point** for the walk is in the Barranco de Vinamar, just outside the village of Morro del Jable. Hotel Río Ventura and Apartamentos Río Maxorata sit on the right-hand side of the mouth of this *barranco*. Take the road up alongside the apartments, following the streambed and, three minutes up, turn off to the right to climb to the Hotel Río Ventura. Our track begins behind this hotel. (It is very likely that future construction will change the layout of this area, but the start of the walk should be easy to locate from this hotel.) Look for the track that climbs above the hotel and follow it all the way up the ridge. Initially the way curves round the hillside to the right, before it strikes off left up the nose of the ridge. A few minutes from the hotel we fork off left and begin the ascent to the peak along a rough and rocky track. A stiff climb lies ahead, but already we have a superb view back over the long white Playa del Matorral with its turquoise-green shoreline. The Barranco de Vinamar, as bleak as the rest of the countryside, cuts straight back into the massif.

Climbing higher, you catch sight of corrals hidden in the depths of the ravine. On rounding to the right-hand side of the ridge, you overlook another harsh valley,

Opposite: From atop Pico de la Zarza — the island's highest peak — you have an eagle's-eye view along the isolated west coast of the Jandía Peninsula. Walk 8 takes you to the stunning beaches of the west.

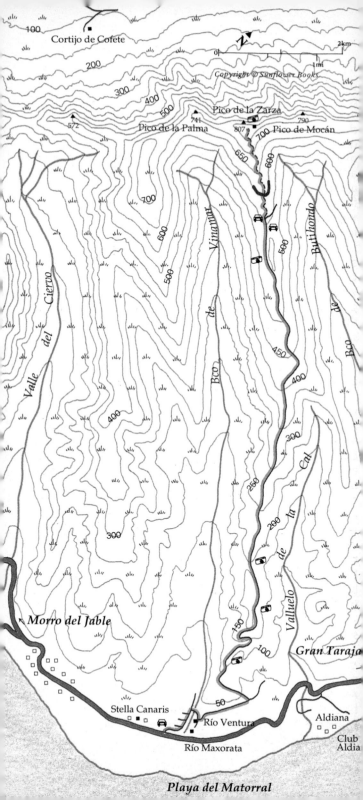

where more ridges hint at a succession of ravines in the distance. Pico de la Zarza is the unimpressive mountaintop that rises a thumbnail above the rest of the massif at the very end of this ridge. Reaching the cloud zone, you discover that the top of the crest is very herbaceous. It's quite a wild garden! Keep well clear of any goats you might encounter up here; they are *very* easily frightened and will dart off in all directions if startled. In particular, avoid any with kids. Just before the track ends, and the final assault, you head alongside a bouldery crest, flooded with *tabaiba* bushes. Look, too, onto the walls below you, to spot some enormous *candelabra*.

The track ends at about **1h15min** into the walk (at the second parking space). The remains of an unused track *do* continue off around the hillside to the right, but we do not: we head straight up to the crest of the ridge, following goats' paths to the summit. Aim for the poles and hut on the peak and take your time. The small piles of stones just serve to confuse you, so ignore them. *Lamarzkia aurea* (it resembles a bottle-brush) flourishes up here. Soon the slopes are ablaze with golden yellow flowers: *Asteriscus*, a pretty furry green-leafed plant.

At **1h35min**, windswept and exhausted, you're on the roof of the island. And what a view! To the left you look across the lofty crags that rupture this impenetrable wall of rock. The jutting southwestern coastline unfolds as this barrier of mountains dies down into sand-patched hills and finally a sea-plain. Don't venture too near to the edge of the peak; it plummets hundreds of feet straight down onto a sea-flat. A mysterious European-style mansion with a turret sits back off the flat in the shadows of the cliffs. This is the Cortijo de Cofete (see Walk 8). More in keeping with the landscape is Cofete, the hamlet of small huts over to the left. To your right stand the high rolling sand hills of the Pared isthmus that joins these mountains to the northern half of the island. On hazeless days you see well down the eastern coastline to Lanzarote in the distance.

Botanists will want to tarry here on the summit for quite some time to discover more of the island's floral treasures: *Echium handiense, Bupleurum handiense, Sideritis massoniana, Argyranthemum winteri,* and the more common *Ranunculus cortusifolius, Andryala cheiranthifolia, Minuartia platyphylla,* and *orobanche.* The summit also houses a tiny meteorological hut.

Home is all downhill — sheer bliss — some hour and a half's descent away.

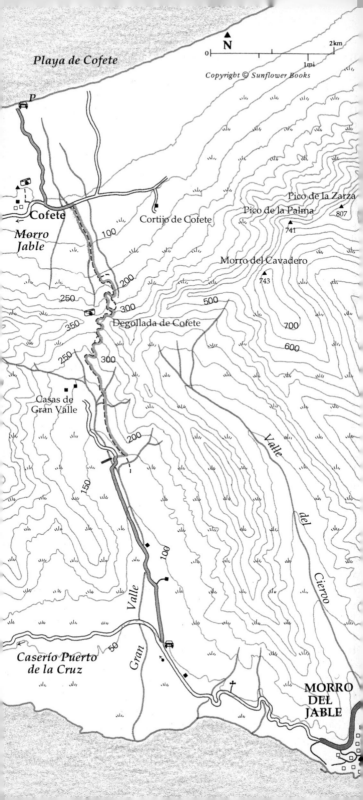

Playa de Cofete

0 N 2km
        1mi

Copyright © Sunflower Books

P

Pico de la Zarza
Pico de la Palma
807

Cofete
Cortijo de Cofete
741

*Morro
Jable*
100

Morro del Cavadero
743

200
250
300

500

350
Degollada de Cofete
700
600

250
300

*Casas de
Gran Valle*

200

Valle

150

100
del

Cierro

Valle

50

*Caserío Puerto
de la Cruz*

Gran

†

**MORRO
DEL
JABLE**

8 BARRANCO GRAN VALLE • DEGOLLADA DE COFETE • PLAYA DE COFETE • BARRANCO GRAN VALLE

Distance: 15km/9.2mi; 3h   Map opposite; photograph page 23

Grade: strenuous. The pass (Degollada de Cofete) costs you a 300m/985ft climb — *twice*. The path on the west coast is rocky and stony. There is some free-wheeling over rocky terrain. It can be very hot, and there is no shade en route. The walk is only recommended for sure-footed experienced hikers with a head for heights.

Equipment: walking boots, warm cardigan, sunhat, raingear, suncream, swimwear, picnic, as much water as you can possibly manage to carry

How to get there and return: use your own transport, or take a taxi to the fork-off up into the Barranco Gran Valle. If the driver doesn't know where it is, it is the ravine beyond Morro del Jable, less than 5km out of the village. Don't forget to ask the driver to return for you!

Cross the Jandía Peninsula to the isolated west coast and see what isolated *really* means! From the crest of the *cumbre* you will have magnificent sweeping views along the beaches of Cofete and Barlovento de Jandía. The empty beaches and crashing breakers are enough to send anyone running down to meet them. Make sure you're fit enough to tackle this hike, however! You may also see the *burros salvajes* — the wild donkeys that roam these hills (twelve of them at the last count, so I'm told). They apparently sneak down to ravage the gardens under cover of night.

A water tank on the left-hand side of the road, just before the Barranco Gran Valle track, is a good landmark for the fork-off into the ravine, where the **walk begins**, 4.5km from Morro del Jable. Standing at the entrance to this austere *barranco*, you can see all the way to the end of it. An abandoned settlement of stone corrals shelters at the foot of the lofty summits. On either side of you the valley floor sweeps back up into severe rocky walls. Out here you meet only goats. Setting off up the track, keep an eye out for the rare cactus-like *Euphorbia handiense* off the side of the track (see page 23). There is quite a colony of it here, and it only grows in a few places south of Morro del Jable. The only other vegetation in this stony terrain is the tobacco plant, *cosco, Lycium intricatum,* and *aulaga*.

Some **5min** along, reach a corral of some substance, with pens constructed out of everything from fishing nets to tin, and anything else they may have scavenged. It even boasts a TV aerial. Keeping left, descend into the streambed, and remain in it until you come to an earthen dam wall with a gaping hole in it (**10min** en route). Here

57

the track swings across in front of the dam, circling it, and then re-enters the *barranco*. Above the dam wall, on your right, you'll see a wide path heading along the hillside. Climb up to it and continue further into the valley. Soon you look out onto the tired stone pens of Casas de Gran Valle, the old pastoral outpost you could see from the outset of the walk. You cross a couple of dry side-streams before the real ascent begins. The path fades now and again, but remains easy to follow.

At the foot of the pass the way swings back to the right to begin a 'Z'. The goats have taken a short-cut and head straight up; we follow them and rejoin the path two minutes up. Small piles of stones help mark the route. This path is now used very seldomly and has crumbled away in parts, but in the past it was the main east—west route across the peninsula. Notice the *Lamarzkia aurea*, the grassy plant flanking the way. Nearing the col, you cross a colourful rock-face bare of vegetation, and the way fades out. Keep to the right-hand side of the pass.

Crossing the pass (Degollada de Cofete), you look up at towering crags that stand like sentries on either side of you. Montaña Fraile is the sharp, pointed peak on the left. Stretching out below you are the striking golden beaches of Cofete (left) and Barlovento de Jandía (right). A chateau-type villa with a turret (so obviously out of place in this bleak landscape) immediately captures your attention. Stories abound about this amazing house, and it still remains shrouded in mystery. It belonged until recently to a Sr Winter, a German who has since died. He came to the island before World War II, and he owned the entire peninsula. When the house was constructed in the early '40s, he forbade his workers (or anyone, for that matter) to reside in Cofete. Everyone had to return to Morro del Jable at the end of the day. And from then on, stories have grown about the place — which would be a good setting for a Hitchcock film! Cofete is the forgotten outpost of stone and cement-block huts you see. The dazzling stretch of coastline detracts from the 'unsympathetic' surroundings.

Your continuation starts off as a good clear path on the right-hand side of the pass, but it rapidly deteriorates. The lichen-flecked pinnacles of rock that pierce this range keep drawing your attention. This chain of volcanic mountains harbours the island's most interesting flora. Five minutes below the pass, notice a faint fork-off to the left that swings down the nose of the crest. Here the main path veers to the right, but we go left to zig-zag down the ridge. It's slippery, but an easier route. Within minutes you will rejoin the main path again. Washed-out sections of the path call for sure foot-work. Not far above the sea-flat, the path crumbles away completely. Here we drop down the side of the ridge, free-wheeling amidst the rock — probably on your backside! Aim for the *barranco* running down on your left and walk down inside it (it's easier than floundering over the rock). On clear days you see the sand dunes of the Pared isthmus falling off into the sea, as well as the hills that enclose Pajara. The *riscos* (cliffs) rise up into dark, sinister shadows behind you.

Accompanied by large, but friendly, yellow grass-hoppers desporting themselves in the *Gramineae*, you will come to a track cutting across in front of you (30 minutes below the pass). Turn left on the track. Cofete certainly is an outpost. The only real 'building' is a bar/restaurant; the rest of the hamlet is a scattering of huts. Wine-red *cosco* provides the only colour in this sun-bleached countryside. Close on **1h20min** into the walk (three minutes along the track), you turn off right to the beach; it lies some ten minutes away. The road to this beach is only accessible (at present) to four-wheel-drive vehicles, which means that you usually share glorious Playa de Cofete with only a few other people. *Beware when you swim:* the water is only safe up to about waist-level; there is a terrific undertow.

Home is back the way we came, over the pass. You turn off the Cofete track at the second *barranco* crossing and head up the streambed. Approaching the ridge, bear left towards it and scramble up the hillside to the path; the rest of the return route is straightforward.

Cortijo de Cofete

Index

Geographical names comprise the only entries in this index; for other entries, see Contents on page 3. **Bold-face** type indicates a photograph; *italic* type indicates a map reference.

Agua de Bueyes 20
Ajuy 14, *49*
Barranco de la Madre del Agua 14, 48, *49*, **50-1**
Barranco de la Peña **48**, *49*, 50, 51
Barranco de las Peñitas 14, **25**, *45*, **47**
Barranco de Pajara **18**
Barranco de Vinamar 53, *54*
Barranco Gran Valle 57
Betancuria 15, 19, **26**
Caldereta 28
Caleta Negra 14, *49*, 51
Casa del Capellán (house) 28
Casas de Jorós 22
Casas de Majanicho *31*, 33, *35*, 36
Casas El Puertito 14, *31*
Casas Puertito de los Molinos 25, 27
Castillo de Rico Roque 29, *34*
Cofete 14, 22, 24, *56*, 59
Colonia García Escamez 27
Corralejo 11, 25, 33, *34*, *37*
   Town plan: touring map
Cortijo de Cofete (house) *54*, 55, *56*, **59**
Costa Calma 11, 16
Cuesta de la Pared 21
Degollada de Cofete 57, 58
Degollada de los Granadillos 18
El Castillo 11, 27
El Cotillo 11, 14, 25, 29, 33, *34*
Embalse de los Molinos 27, 41, *42*, **44**
Ermita de Nuestra Señora de la Peña 18, *45*, 46, **47**
Faro de Jandía 22
Faro de Tostón *34*, **35**
Giniginamar 11, 21
Gran Tarajal 15, 20
   Town plan: touring map
Gran Valle 22, **23**, *56*, 57
Huertas de Chilegua (valley) 16
Jandía (peninsula) 22, **23**, 27, *56*, 57

La Antigua 15, 20
La Lajita 11
La Matilla 25, 27
La Oliva 19, 25, 28
La Pared 15, 16, 59
Lajares 28, 29, 33
Las Playitas 11, 15, 21
Llanos de la Concepción 41, *42*
Lobos 14, 30-2, *31*, **32**
Los Canarios 15
Los Molinos 27
Montaña Quemada 27
Montaña Tindaya 25, 28, **38**, *39*, **40**
Morro de la Cueva 41, 43
Morro del Jable 11, 15, 22, 24, 52, *54*, *56*, 57
   Town plan: touring map
Pájara 14, 17, 18, **19**, 45
Parque Holandés 27
Peña Horadada (rock) **48**, *49*, 51
Pico de la Zarza **52**, 53, *54*, *56*
Playa de Barlovento de Jandía 14, 24
Playa de Cofete 14, *56*, 57, 59
Playa de la Calera 14, *31*
Playa del Matorral *54*
Playa de Sotavento de Jandía 14, 15, **17**, 21
Pozo Negro 27
Presa de las Peñitas 18, *45*
Puerto de la Cruz 23
Puerto de la Peña 14, 16, 48, *49*
Puerto del Rosario 11, 20, 25, 27
   Town plan: touring map
Punta de Jandía 22, 23
Tarajalejo 11, 15, 21
Tefía 27
Tetir 27
Tindaya 25, 28, 38, *39*
Tuineje 20
Vega de Río de Palmas 14, 19, 45, *45*